Modeling Military Miniatures

Tips, Tools, & Techniques

Kim Jones

Schiffer Publishing Ltd
77 Lower Valley Road, Atglen, PA 19310

Dedication

This book is dedicated to the memory of my father, Jay L. Jones, whose photograph appears on the cover. His inspiration and encouragement have been invaluable over the years and I could never begin to thank him enough.

Book Design by Audrey L. Whiteside

Printed in China

ISBN: 0-88740-883-4

Library of Congress Cataloging in Publication Data

Jones, Kim, 1954-
Modeling military miniatures : tips, tools & techniques / Kim Jones.
p. cm.
ISBN 0-88740-883-4 (paper)
1. Miniature craft. 2. Military miniatures. 3. Models and model making. I. Title.
TT178.J66 1995
745.592'82--dc20 95-24446
CIP

Contents

Published by Schiffer Publishing, Ltd.
77 Lower Valley Road
Atglen, PA 19310
Please write for a free catalog.
This book may be purchased from the publisher.
Please include $2.95 postage.
Try your bookstore first.

We are interested in hearing from authors with book ideas on related subjects.

Prologue

There is a sequential thought process that should be followed when creating a military miniature. Sometimes it is difficult to decide what step should follow the one that you have just completed. It is important for the sculptor to know when it is more expedient to sculpt a certain part on the figure or to actually construct that part separately and apply it at a later stage. With practice, you will be able to determine these steps with ease.

The ability to sculpt your own military miniatures, however, is merely a single step in the creation of finished, well displayed pieces. In some instances a commercial casting may become the basis for a conversion, creating something completely different from the original. I will show you how to convert a casting of a World War II Cossack into a U.S. Cavalry Trooper of the 1880s.

While converting the Cossack into a Cavalryman, I will suggest ways to improve commercial castings to make them appear more natural, so that they will be truly one-of-a-kind pieces. I will also show you how to solve particular sculpting problems and offer techniques for making accessories. I will give you some specific tips that will make the sculpting process quicker and easier as well.

Whether you sculpt your own figure or convert and paint a commercial miniature, you will want to display your completed piece in a manner that is best suited to your particular figure. In the following pages, I will help you decide on an appropriate setting and I will also show you how to create that setting so that your figure will represent an actual slice of history.

Sources

Verlinden Productions — WWII Cossack
Available from your local hobby shop or directly from VLS, 811 Lone Star Drive, O'Fallon, MO 63366, USA.

A & B Epoxy Putty — Available at your local hobby shop and hardware store, or contact Mike Davidson at The Hussar, 6029 S. Sheridan, Tulsa, OK 74145, USA. (918) 492-3559.

I invite questions or comments on any segments of this book. Please send all letters to Kim Jones, c/o Schiffer Publishing Ltd., 77 Lower Valley Road, Atglen, PA 19310.

Preparations

Tools of the Trade

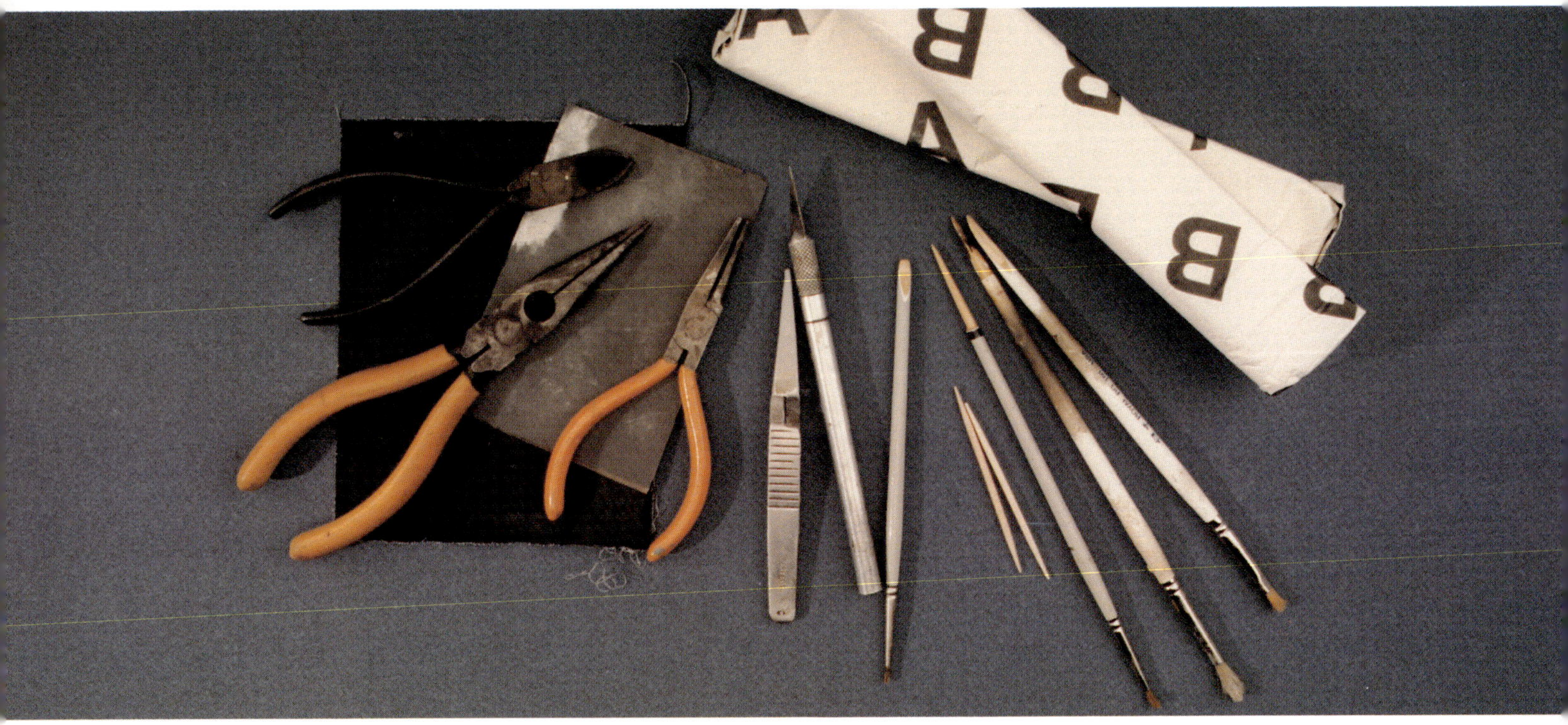

A few of the tools used in the sculpting of military miniatures, for the converting of commercial castings. While some of them are available at your local hardware store, others you will have to make yourself. Illustrated are (from right to left) emory cloth, sandpaper, diagonal cutters for cutting wire and sprues, needle-nose pliers and ring pliers for bending wires, tweezers, an X-acto knife, toothpicks, several tools of my own design fashioned from paint brushes, and two part epoxy putty (marked A & B) which we use to sculpt the figure itself.

This is the tool I use the most in sculpting. It is used for making folds in clothing.

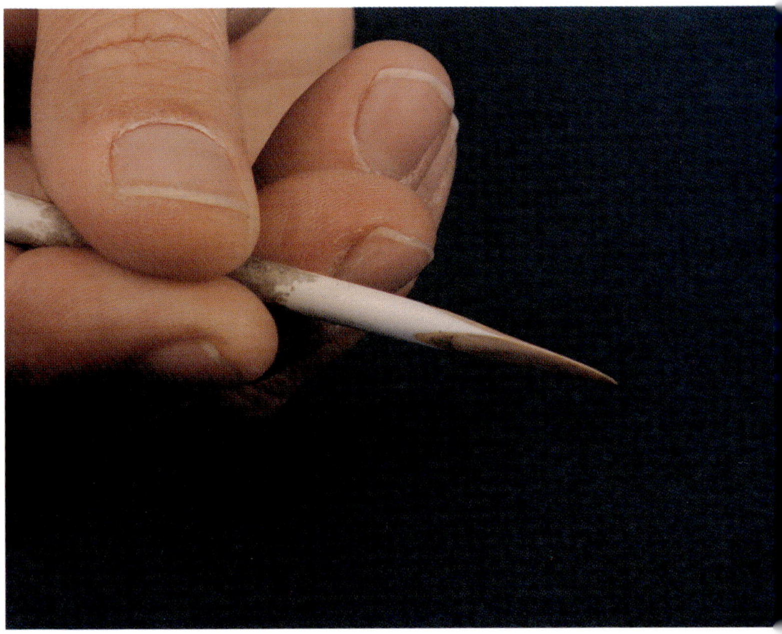

This is basically the same type of tool but it has more of a knife edge for finer wrinkles.

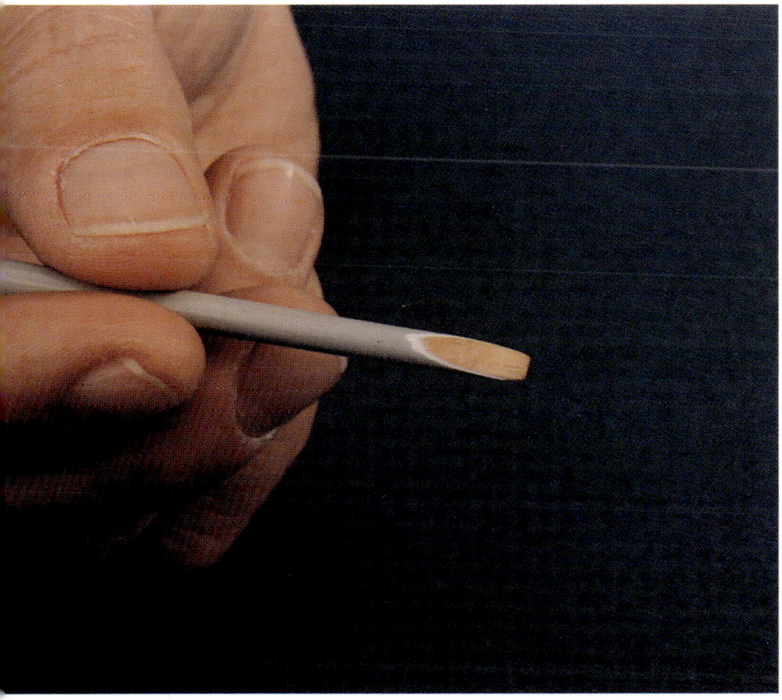

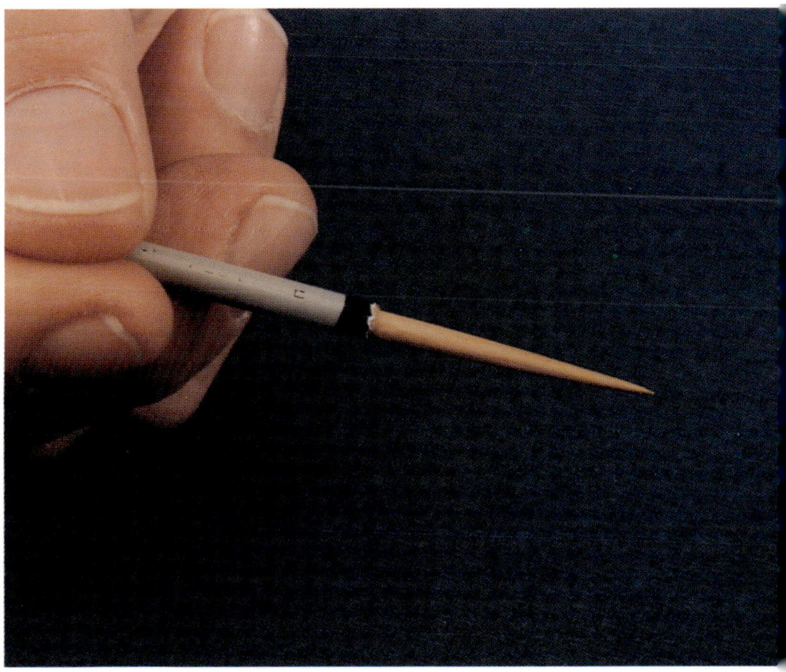

This chisel shaped tool is used for making small, shallow wrinkles, for outlining belts, and for adding seam lines.

This stylus-shaped tool is primarily for rolling out the putty on the initial armature and for making folds and wrinkles. The point can be used also for texturing hair or fur clothing items.

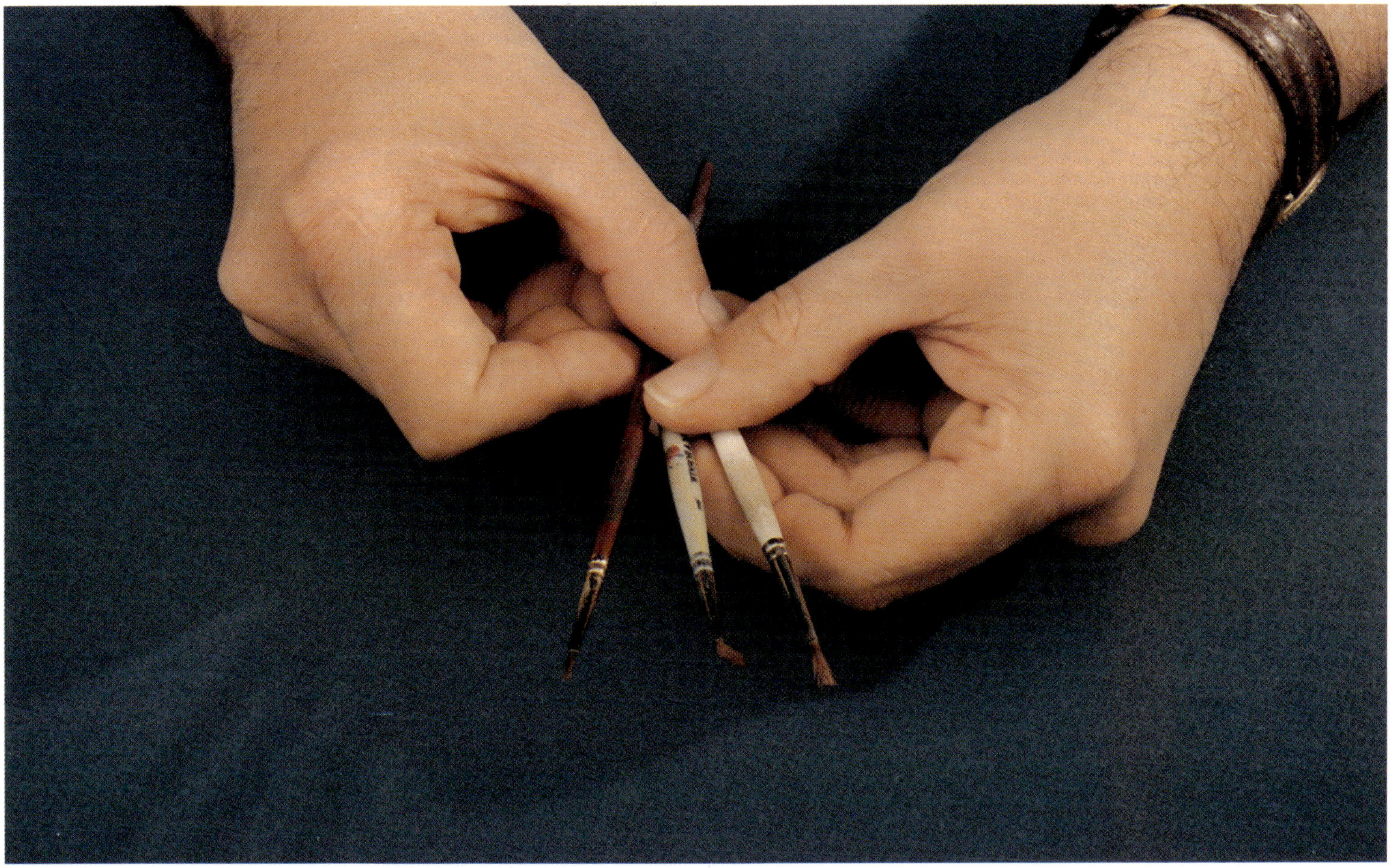

While old, worn paint brushes can no longer be used for painting they have yet to outlive their usefulness. They are the basic stock from which I make the tools just described. I use paint brush handles to make my tools. The tool shape and size depends on the size of figures on which you are working.

To make the knife-edged tool that I use most, use an X-acto knife to shave down both sides of the paint brush shaft; carve a sharp edge along one side and a rounded edge on the other, creating a butter knife blade of sorts.

After carving, the tip should appear as a triangular shape.

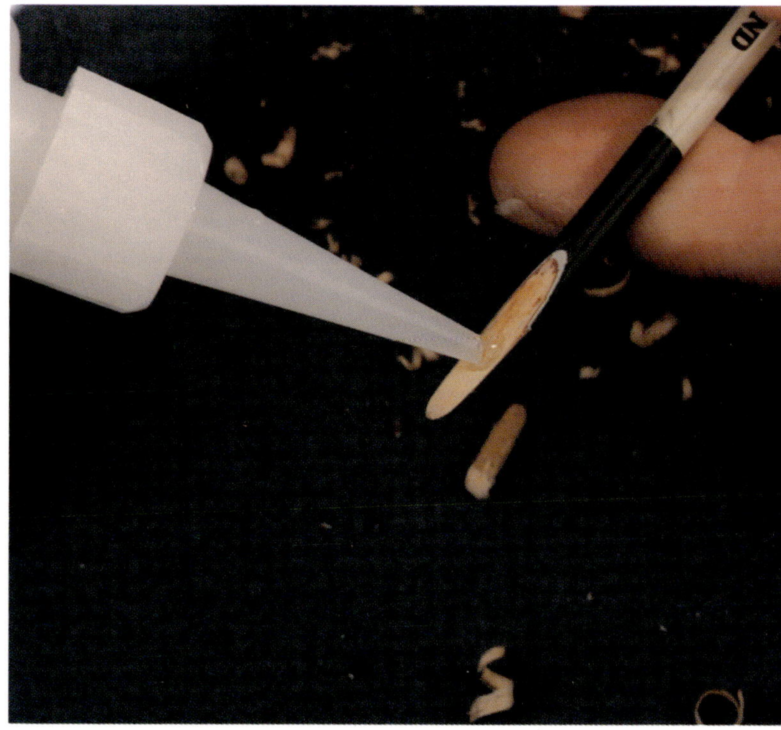

Round off the tip with sand paper to make it more like a butter knife. We are rounding the knife edge and not the dull side. Then sand the rest of the blade smooth, removing all knife marks and rough grain. Coat the tool with Super Glue to give it a smooth surface and to keep the epoxy putty from sticking to the tool.

Sand the coated surface of the tool with fine grit sand paper to make sure that it is completely smooth. The final product.

All of the tools are constructed in this manner; however, there are specialized tools you can make for specific sculpting situations and we will cover these later in the book.

Converting a Commercial Casting

For this project I want to take a look at converting a commercial casting into a figure of my choice. Since I am primarily interested in sculpting figures of the U.S. cavalry during the Indian Wars, I am always on the lookout for figures that can be easily "conscripted" into the American service. I have chosen a Verlinden Productions 120mm Kuban Cossack of World War II to convert to a U.S. cavalryman of the mid-1880s.

To begin with, remove all sprues and pour plugs from the casting.

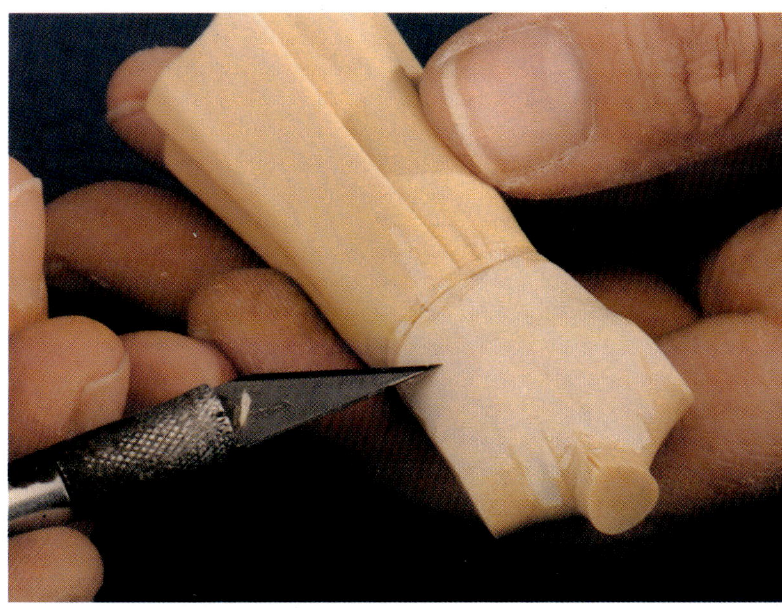

Glue the torso to the lower part of the body for ease of handling before carving off the unwanted parts of the figure. Once the torso is glued, remove all ornamentation from the front of the jacket with a sharp blade. Do not worry about taking off too much material as we will be building up the front of the jacket with putty. I have cleaned off the front of the jacket, including the folds which will be sculpted on later.

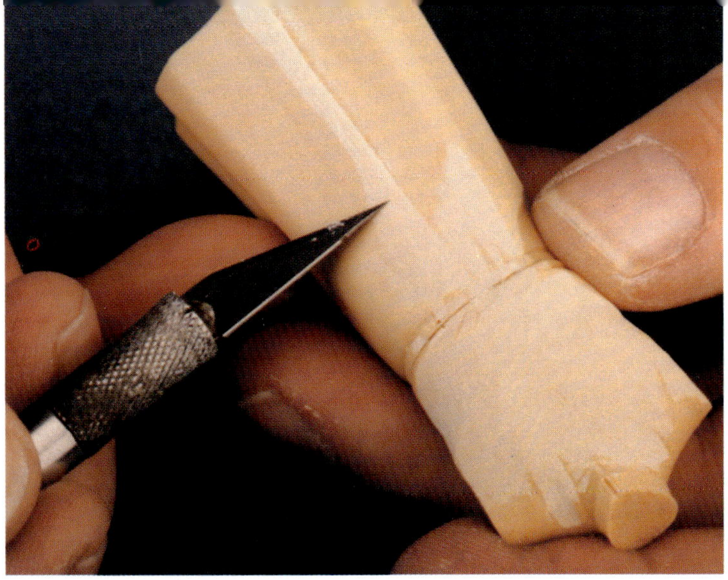

I am carving off part of the original coat opening. This coat is single breasted, mine will be double breasted. While I am using an X-acto knife here, a grinder or files will work just as well. Whatever gets you from point A to point B. While it is not necessary to remove all of the bottom of the coat opening as it will be covered with putty later, we do want to remove all of the top.

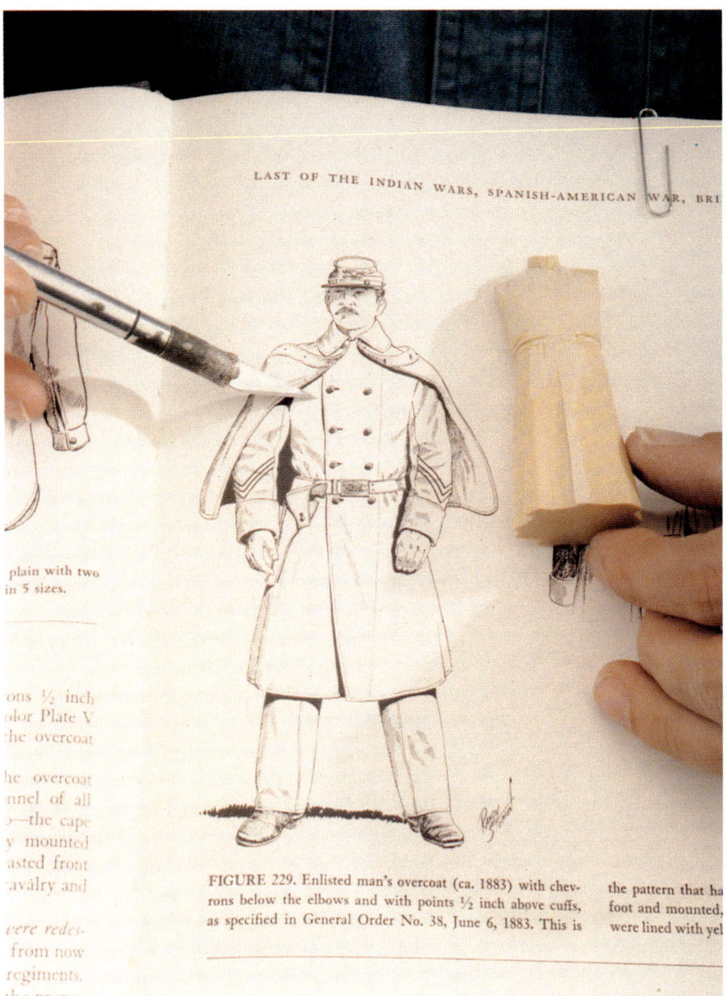

While remodeling clothes or uniforms, it is critical to refer to your reference material so that you are aware of where you have been and where you are going.

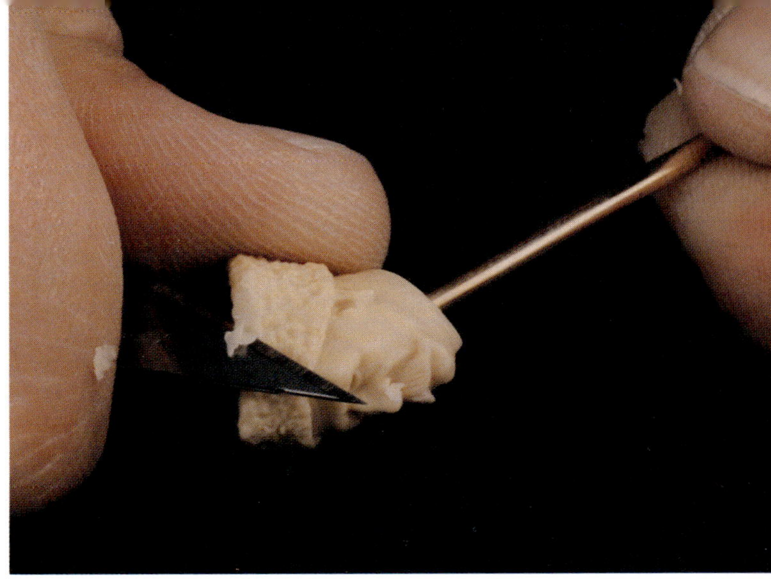

The next step is to work on the head. Our figure will be wearing a kepi. After clean up I have mounted the head on a wire to aid in the shaping of the hat.

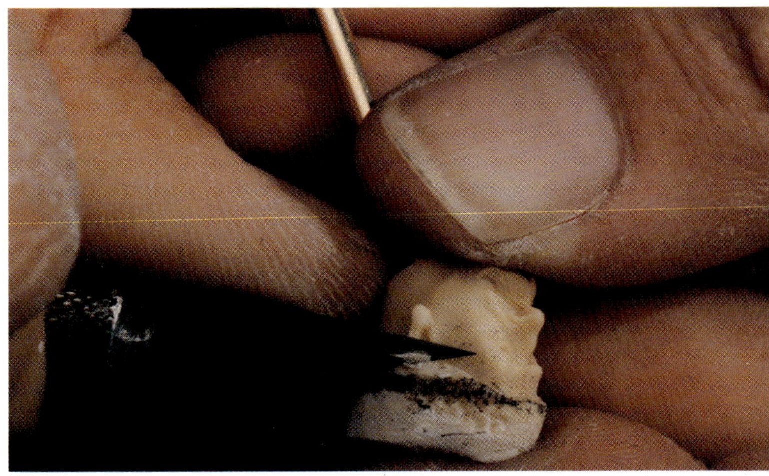

After partially carving down the existing hat, I take a pencil and mark where the new lower edge of the hat will be. This guide line will remind me not to carve off too much material from the area of the kepi. Enough material must also be left to resculpt the top of the ear.

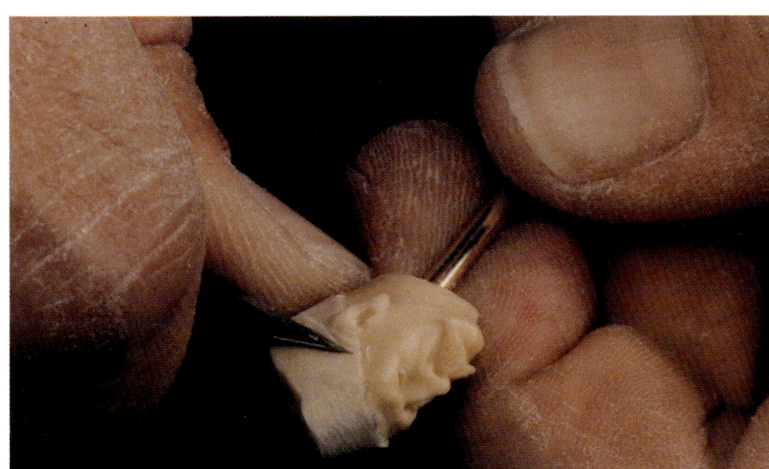

With the X-acto knife, carefully remove the existing material from around the ears.

This is the finished recarved ear and while we have lost our line indicating the bottom of our kepi, it was necessary to get it out of the way to carve the entire ear. After carving off the excess resin, I polished away the carving marks with fine steel wool. Continue the same process on the right ear. When carving the ears, be sure that the tops of the ears are in line with the eyes.

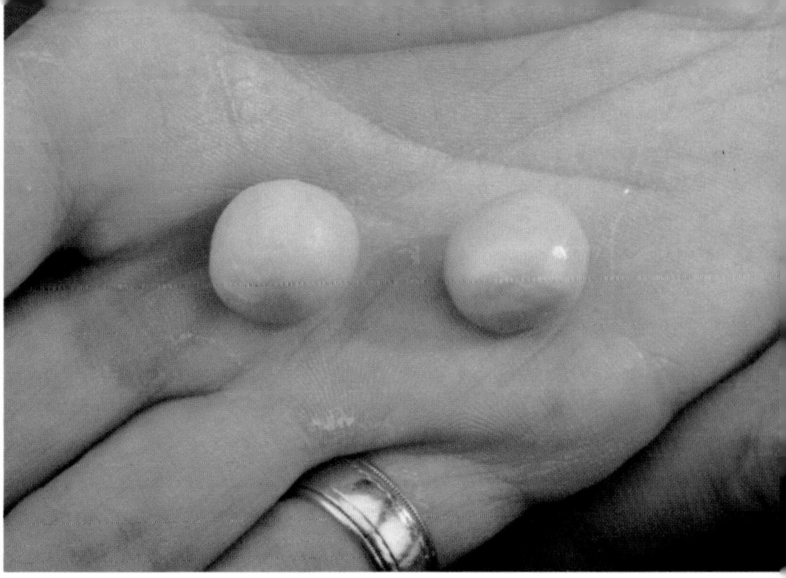

To insure a 50/50 mix, roll equal-sized balls of putty. In this photo the A is on the left and the B is on the right. You will notice that each is a slightly different color from the other. When you knead the two together, you can be assured of a proper mix when the color is uniform. You have about 45 minutes of working time before the putty becomes too hard to sculpt, so only mix up as much as you can use in that time.

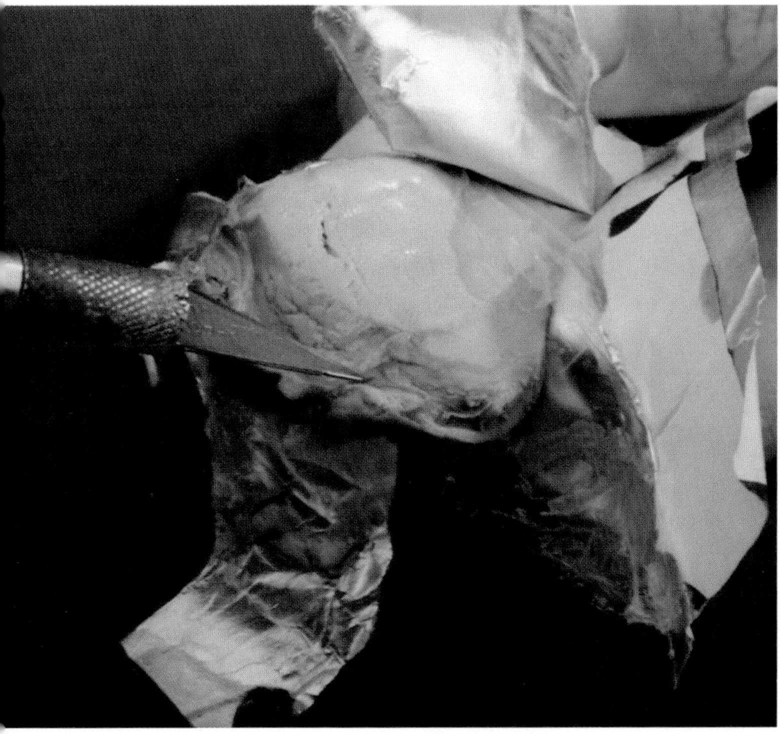

Now we're ready to begin to apply putty, changing the shape of the coat from single-breasted to double-breasted. When mixing part A with part B of the epoxy putty, you want to use equal amounts of both and knead them thoroughly until the mixed putty has a consistent color throughout. When opening a new package of putty, or if your opened putty has been exposed to the air for any length of time, the B part of the putty may have formed a brown residue. You either want to peal that brown residue off and throw it away or, when dividing your putty up into equal amounts, knead the B part by itself until its color becomes uniform again and the residue has disappeared. While it is important to use a 50/50 putty mixture, if you are going to favor one over the other, be sure to use more A than B. A is the hardener and B is the resin.

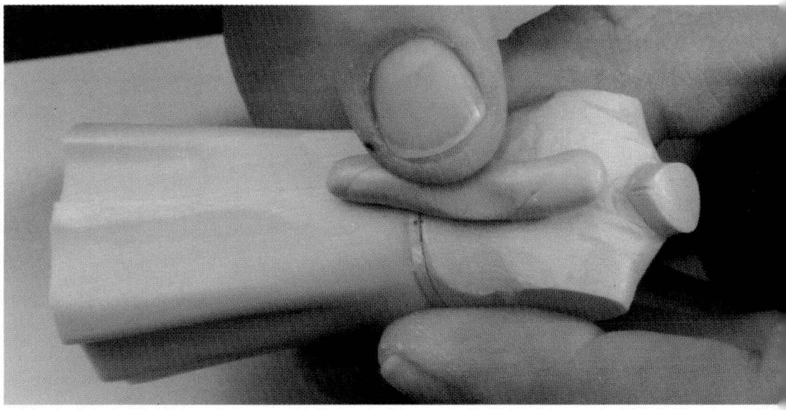

Apply a snake of putty to the front of the coat.

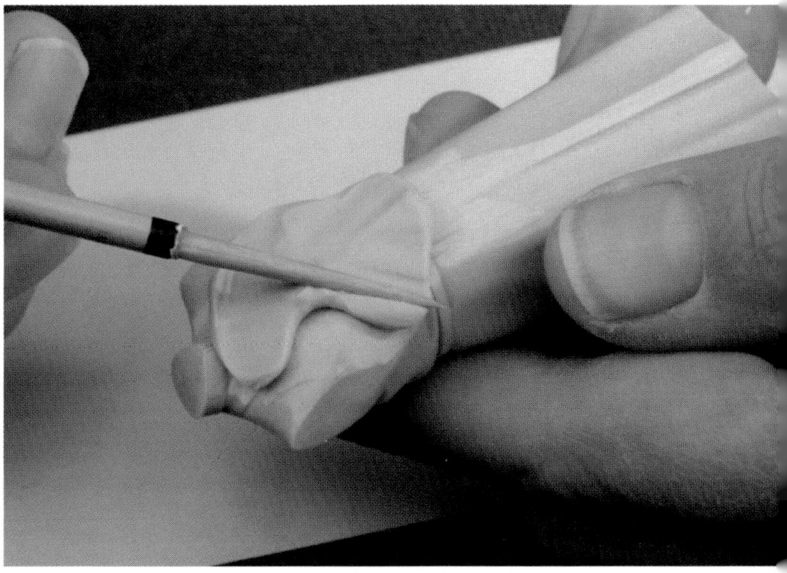

With a round, pointed tool or a toothpick, roll out the putty to cover the area where you removed the detail previously.

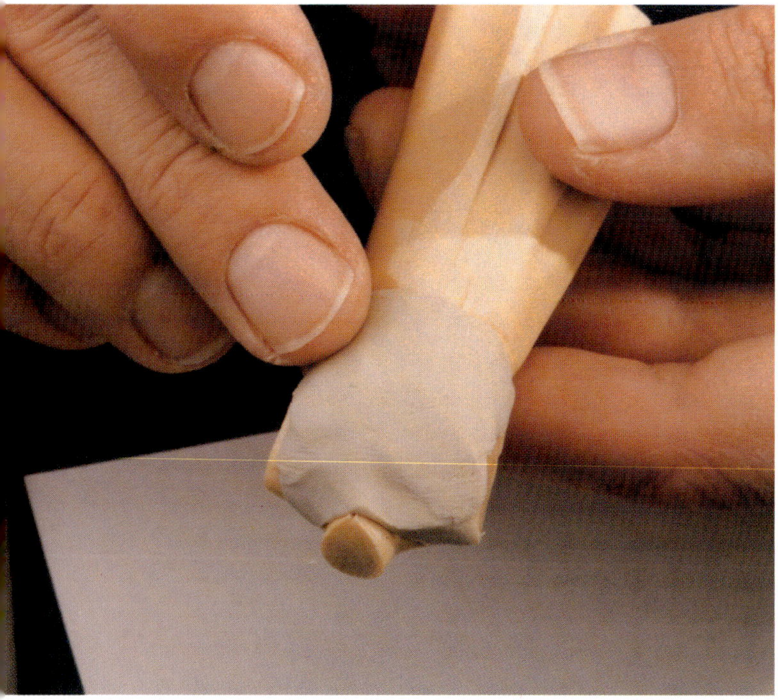

When working with the putty, keep water or lacquer thinner on hand in which to dip the tools to keep them from sticking to the putty. Here I am spreading the putty with my finger and smoothing it at the same time.

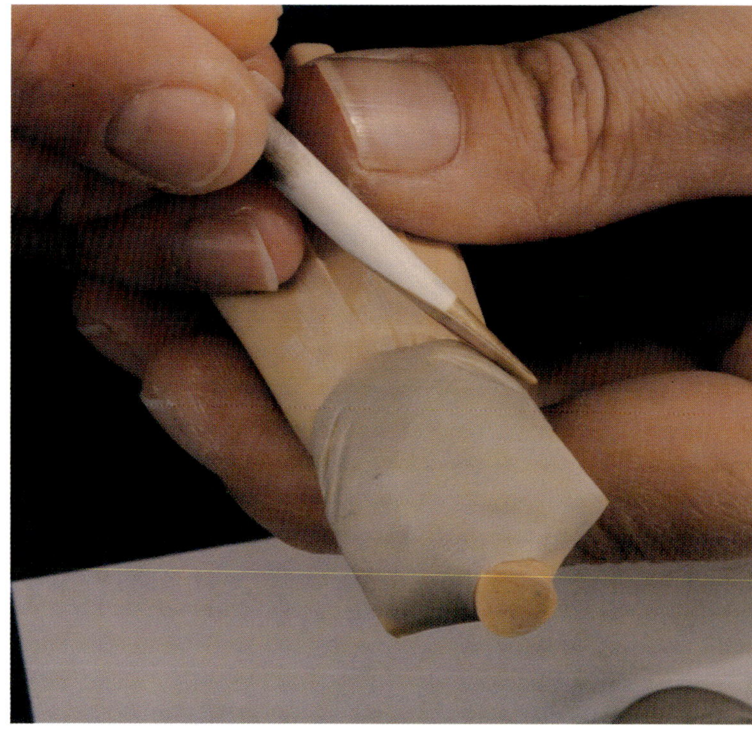

Begin the sculpting process with folds first, using the tool we carved above. Seam lines and the closure of the coat will be added later. For the beginning sculptor, it is important to study the way wrinkles fall in particular types of clothing and under certain conditions. There are books available that show different types of clothing wrinkles. You may also simply enlist the aid of a family member or friend to model particular types of clothing in the appropriate postions. A Poloroid camera comes in handy. Don't keep your friends and family standing in one position for very long at one time.

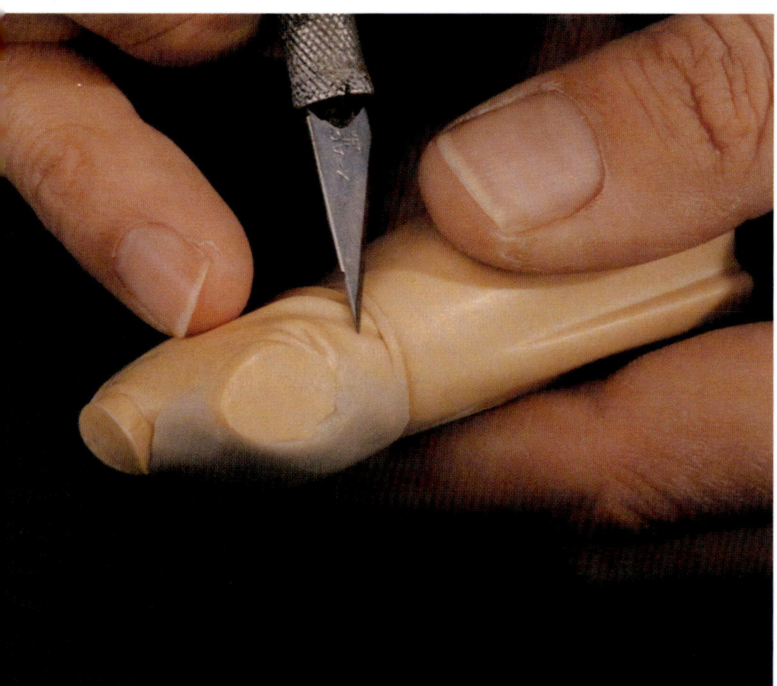

Since we are not altering the back of the figure, we want to smooth the putty out where the front meets the back of the figure so that there is a smooth transition between front and rear.

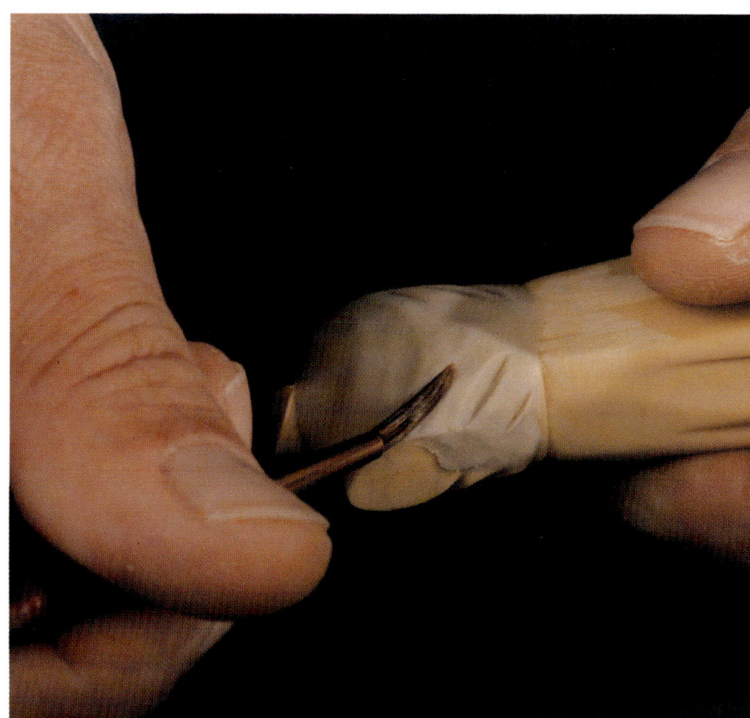

Take a fine pointed brush and smooth out the impressions you made with the tool.

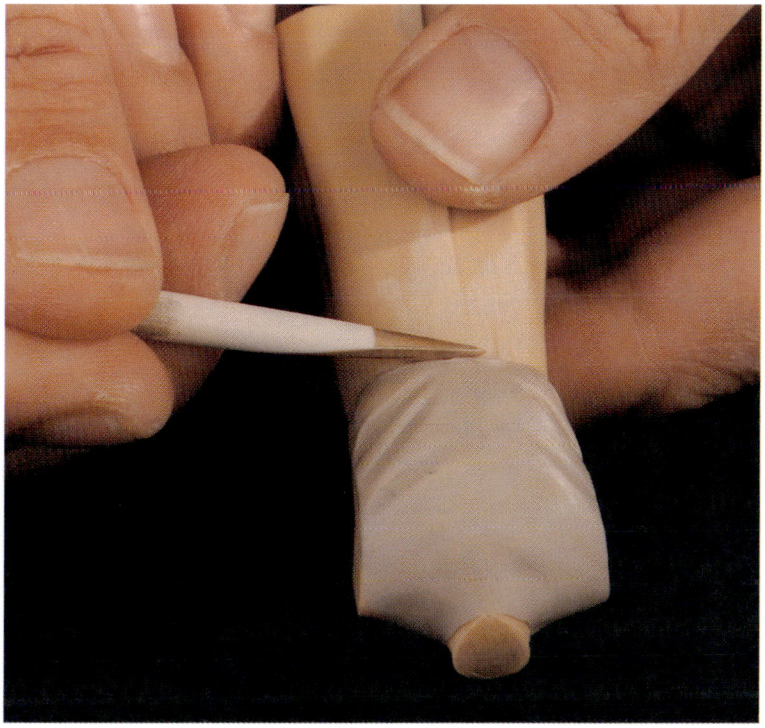

Our figure has a belt over his coat. You want to push the putty up where the belt will go underneath the coat and then smooth out the line with a brush as we did before.

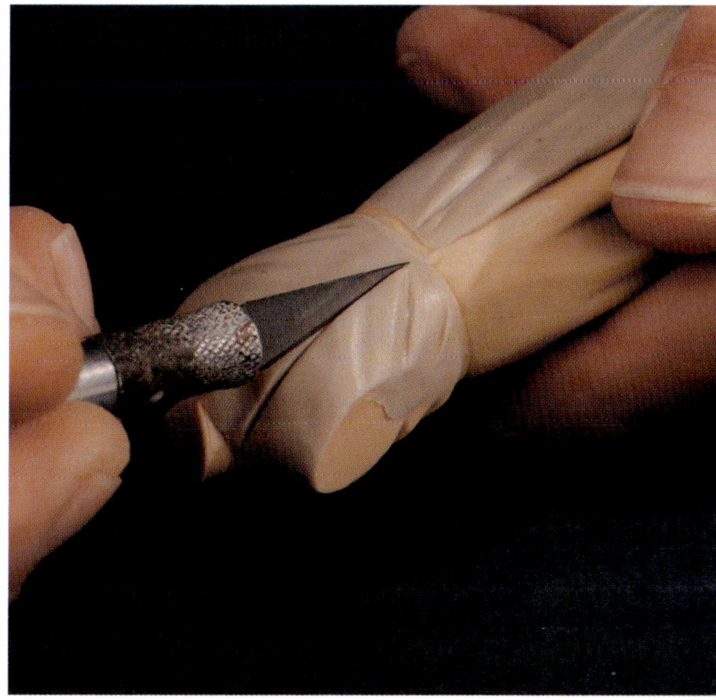

Continue to define the opening of the coat with the knife-edge tool, creating somewhat of an undercut. Smooth out the wrinkles with a brush.

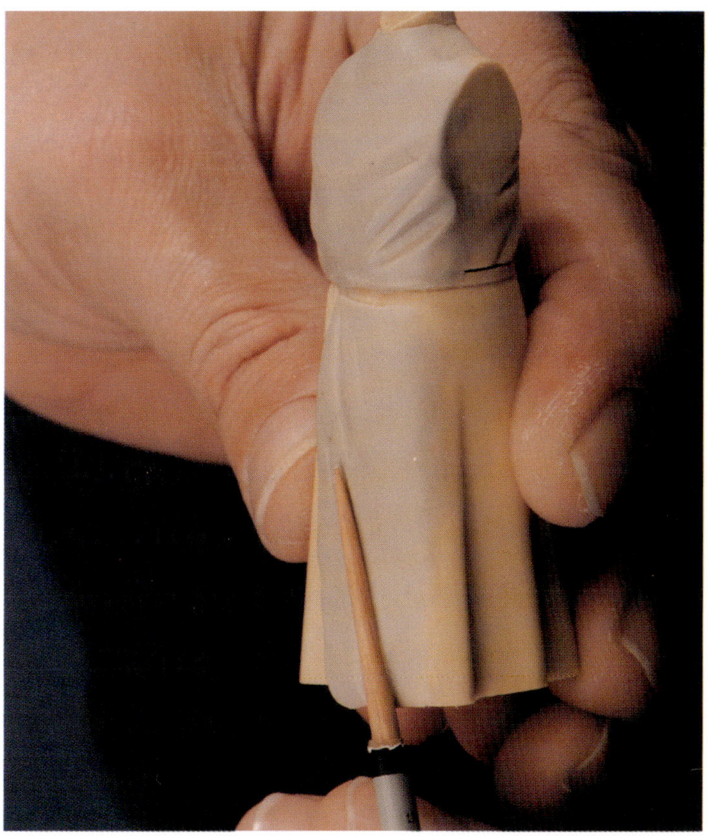

Now we'll lay on putty for the bottom portion of the coat that falls below the intended belt line. Again, work toward the backside of the figure, creating a smooth transition between the front and back. Once the putty is smooth, begin applying folds in the lower portion of the coat.

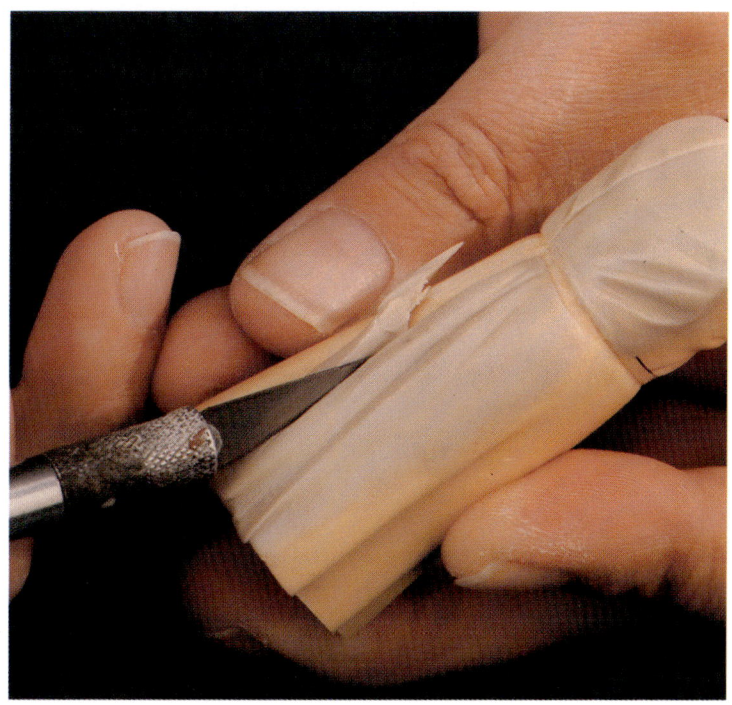

While outlining the lower opening of the coat, you will be removing some of the putty. Set it aside and save it for later.

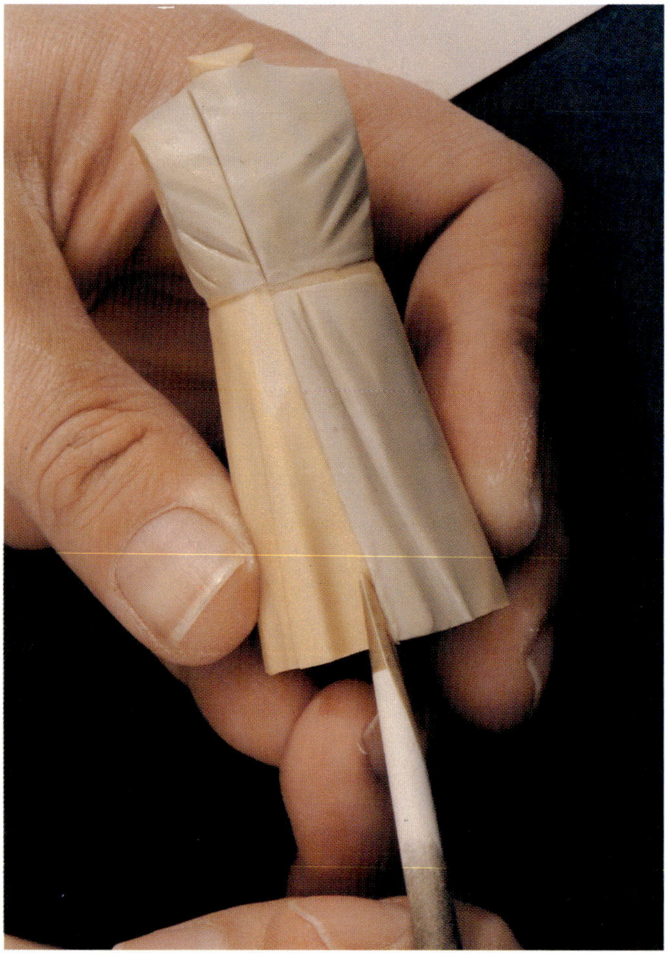

Deliniate the opening of the coat using the sharp blade of an X-acto knife.

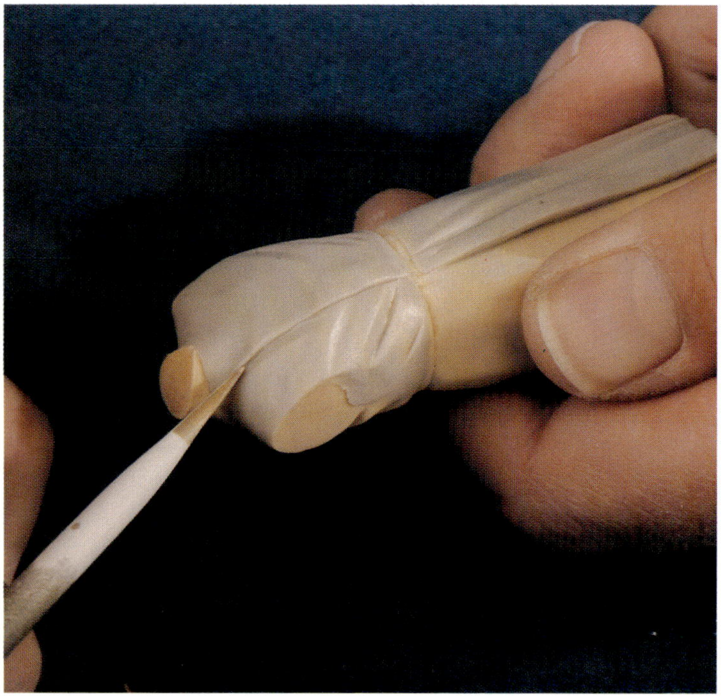

Begin the same undercutting process with the knife-edge tool along the top portion of the coat. Again smooth out your work with a brush.

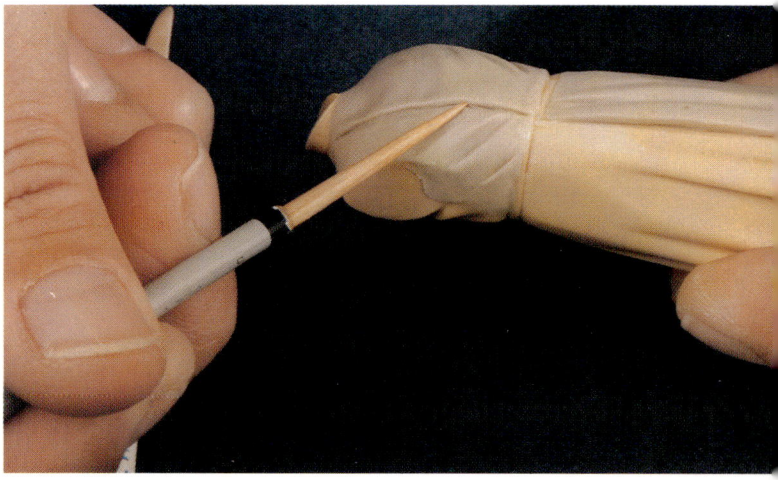

Go back and redefine the wrinkles you created earlier that were affected by the undercutting of the opening of the coat. Clean up again with the brush. Constantly recheck your reference material to insure that you obtain the proper look of the uniform.

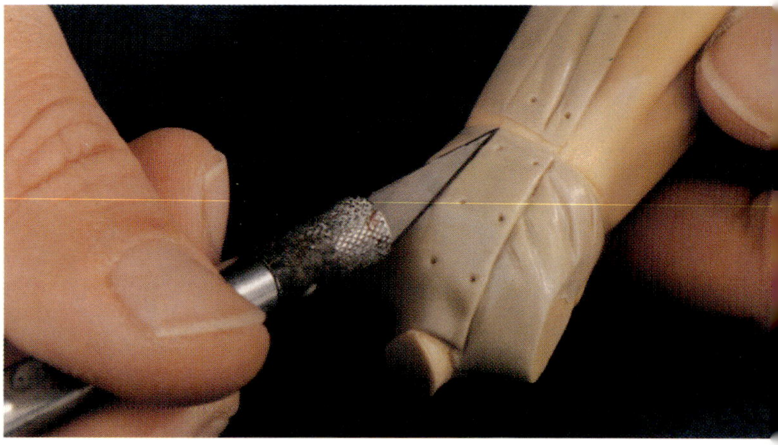

Establishing the location of the buttons with the pointed tool or a toothpick. Using the X-acto knife, establish the seam line.

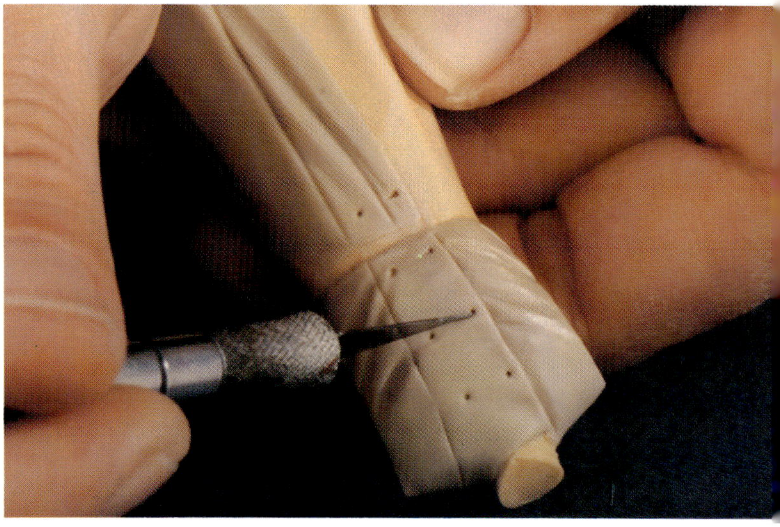

For the buttons that actually close the coat, we give the indication of the button hole using the tip of the X-acto knife.

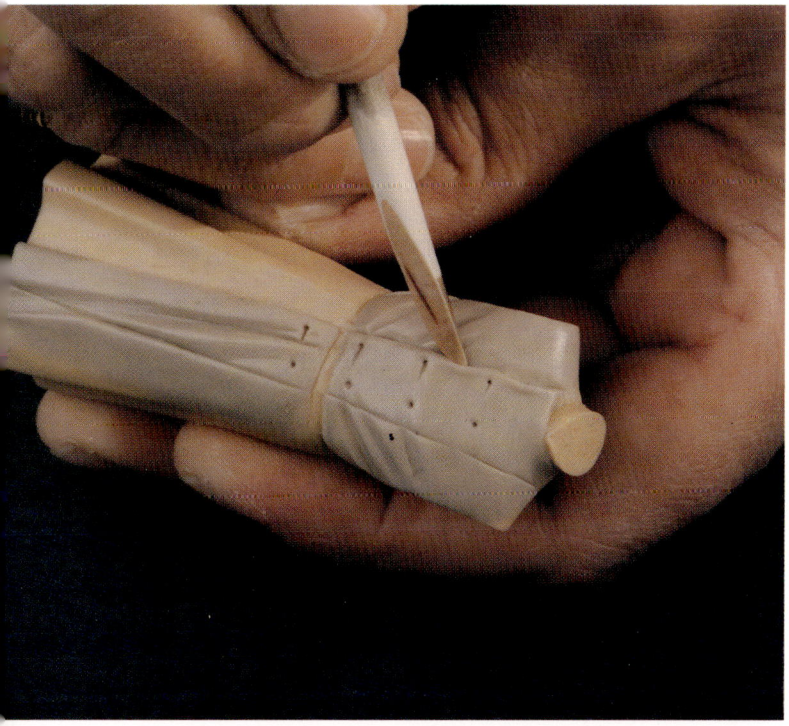

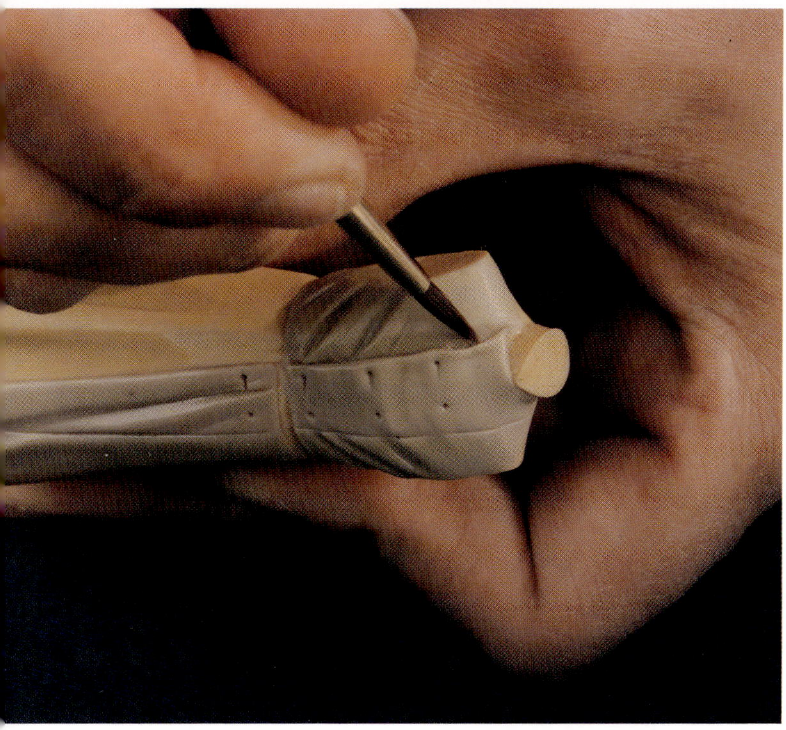

Using the knife-edged tool or the X-acto knife, blouse out the enclosure of the coat with a lifting motion, blousing it only between the buttons. Smooth out with a paint brush.

Create a few small, tight wrinkles with the knife-edge tool where the belt will gather the material of the coat. This piece is ready for the oven.

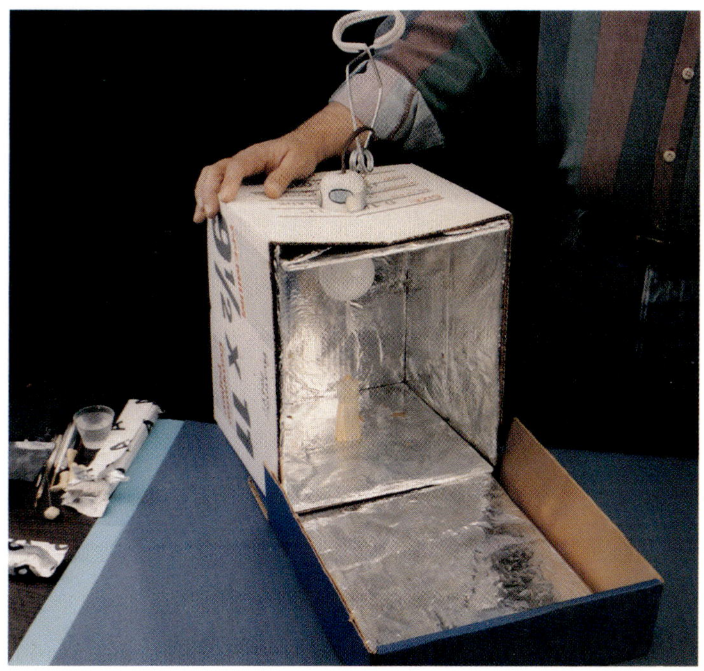

Speaking of the oven, while you can use your home oven on the lowest heat setting, I prefer to use a home made oven of my own construction. It is simply a computer paper box lined with tin foil which has a hole cut in the top. A light fixture with a 75 to 100 watt bulb is inserted into the hole. Here is the assembled box with the figure in it ready for baking. Be careful when using an oven of this sort. It can get very hot, between 120 and 150 degrees. This oven will harden the putty in approximately 15 minutes. If left on its own, it takes about 8 hours for the epoxy putty to cure. I do not recommend that you leave your figure in for more than 15 or 20 minutes because the putty will continue to cook, can darken and will become brittle. If it is a resin figure you are converting, prolonged baking can also soften the resin or cause uncured resin in the center of the figure to cook out. It is difficult to paint over that uncured resin.

Next I drilled out the neck on the body to accept the cut down rod that was inserted into the head earlier. We can now glue the head into place.

I attached the head at an angle to provide a little more interest. Taking a ball of putty, apply it to the head to begin to form the kepi.

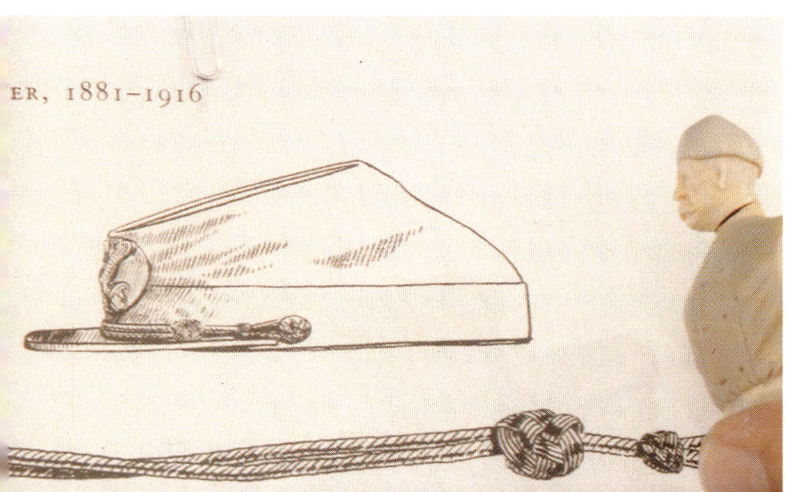

It is not necessary to be concerned with keeping the putty off the ears at the moment as we will be trimming off the bottom of the kepi. This is the shape of the kepi.

We'll add a couple of slight compression wrinkles to the kepi and then smooth them out with a brush.

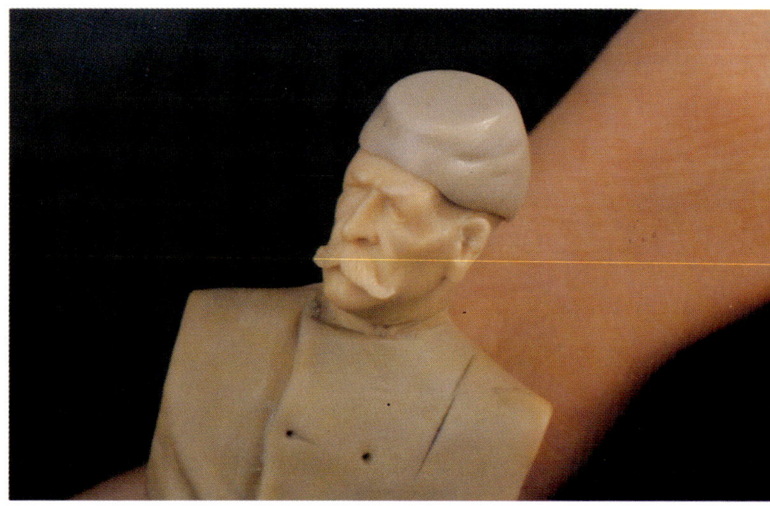

The smoothed wrinkles.

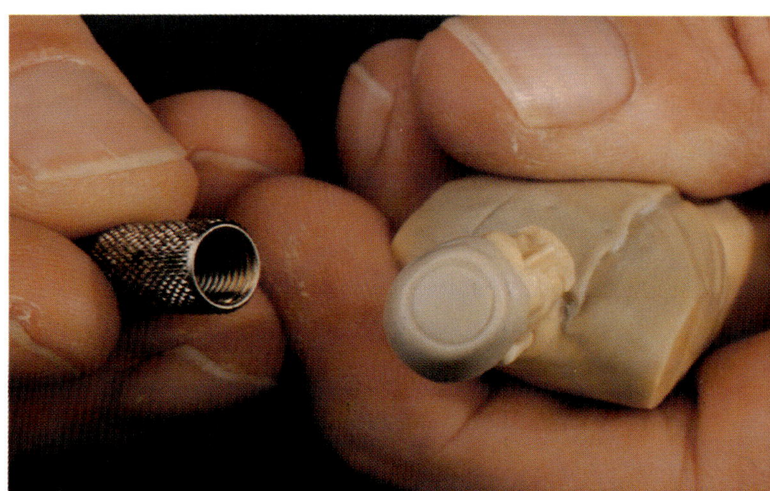

Looking around at my tools, I had to come up with a round object that would create the seam where the body of the kepi meets the top. While you could use the proper sized brass or aluminum tubing, the end of my pen vice was exactly the right size. The result.

Using the sharp edge of my X-acto knife I press in the seam that runs around the body of the kepi.

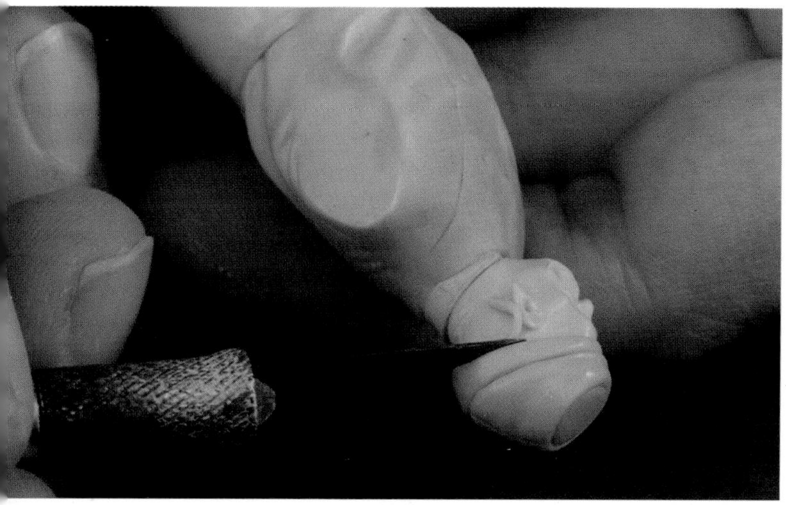

Trim off the bottom of the cap using the X-acto knife.

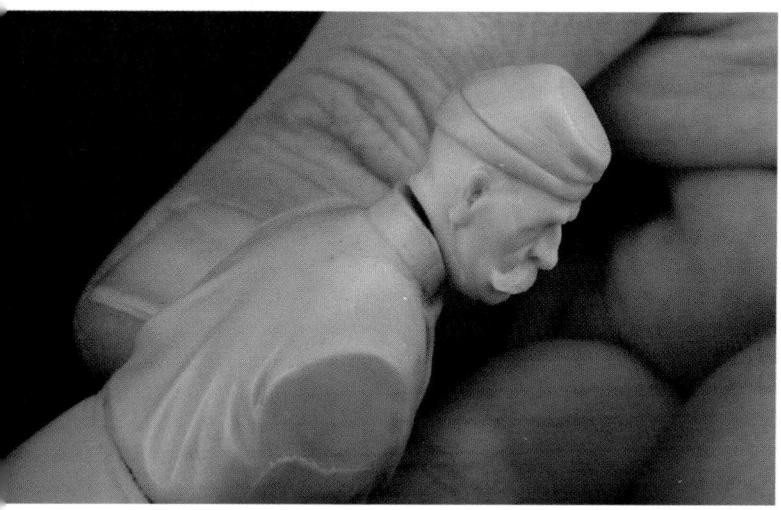

The result. Put this in the oven to bake now for fifteen minutes. It is best when working on different parts of the figure that you bake one part before moving on to another. This way you avoid destroying the work you have already done.

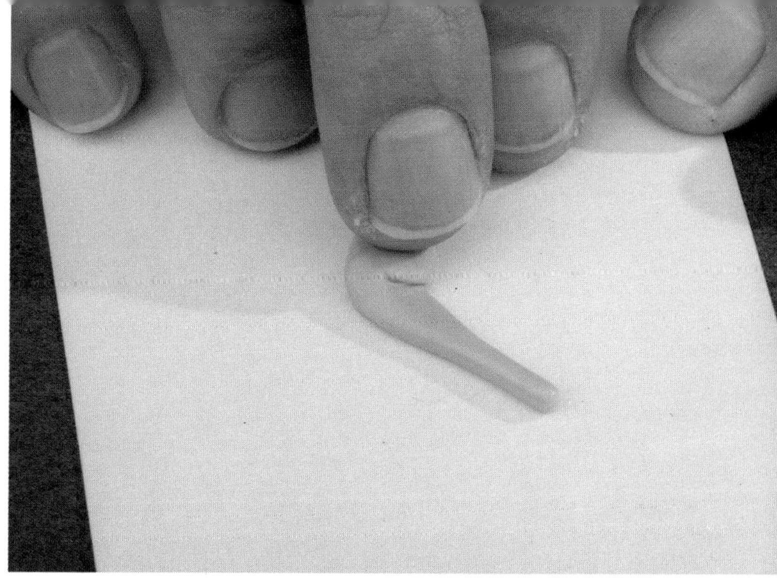

While we're waiting for the figure to bake in the oven we can roll out a length of putty to begin construction of the holster. Again refer to your reference material for the proper shape and size. The holster begins to take shape.

Using your X-acto knife, trim the holster to shape. The final shape of the holster. We will add the flap and the pistol handle after this part has hardened in the oven.

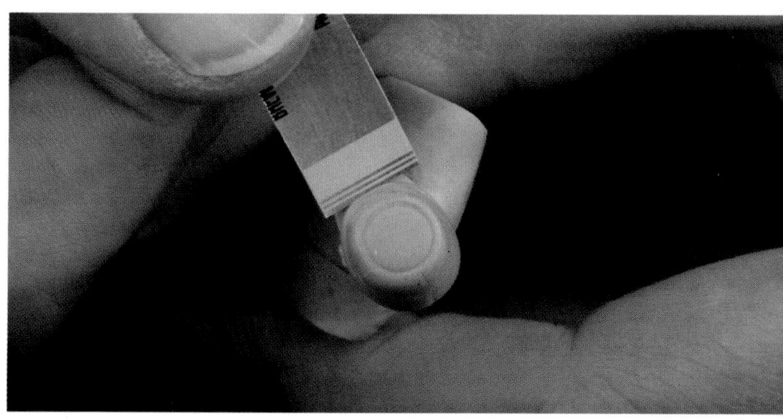

Using an aluminum beverage can, we cut a piece of aluminum for the kepi bill. I've found this to be the best material to use because it can easily be bent and yet it retains its rigidity and shape. If you need the bill to be thicker, just add a layer of epoxy putty. Sizing the bill to insure that it is the proper width.

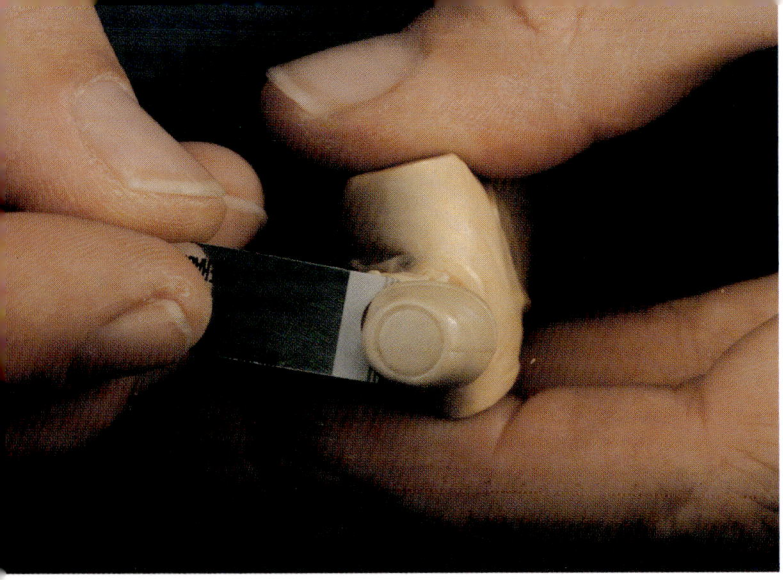

From one end we cut out a circular area that will fit against the forehead. Scissors will work. The circumference of the circle is not all that critical at this point as long as it will go around the head. Test fit and then trim if necessary.

The resulting bill, ready to be applied.

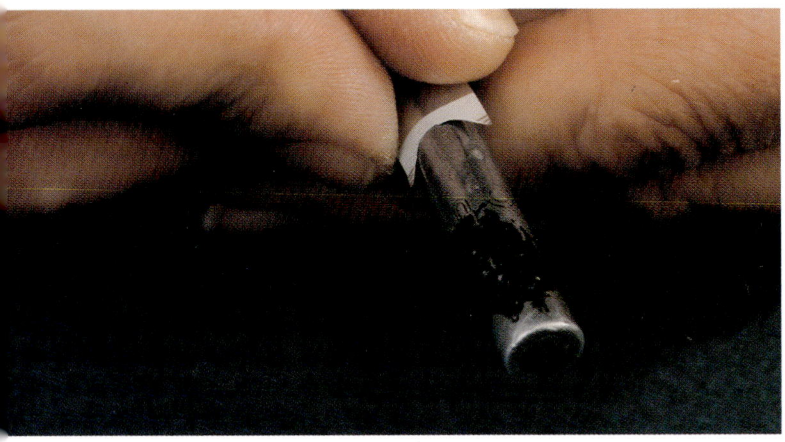

Put a slight bend in the bill by bending it over the handle of an X-acto knife. Don't make the bend too radical, this is a kepi, not a baseball cap.

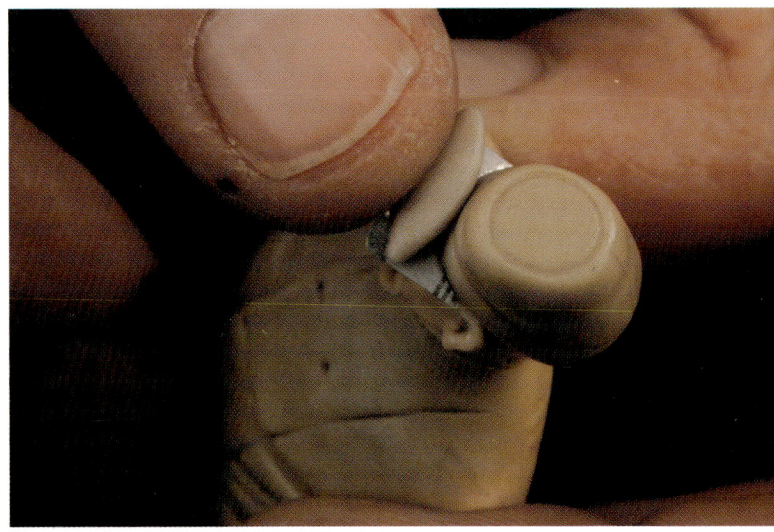

Glue the bill in place with Super Glue. Add a thin layer of putty to the bill to thicken it.

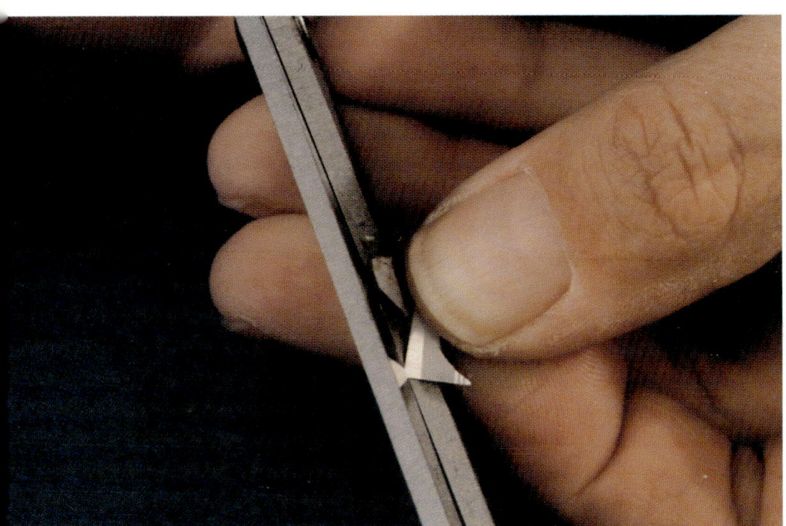

Trim the bill to length and round the corners of the bill with scissors, sandpaper, or both.

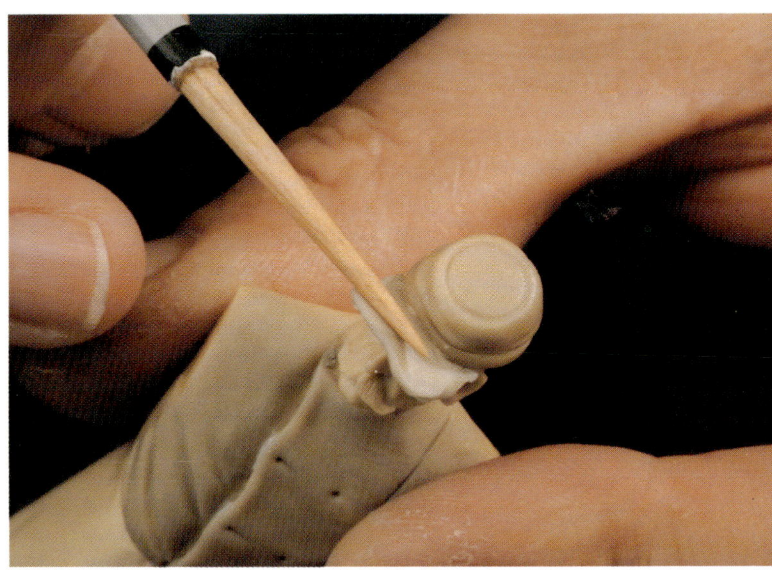

Thinning the putty over the bill.

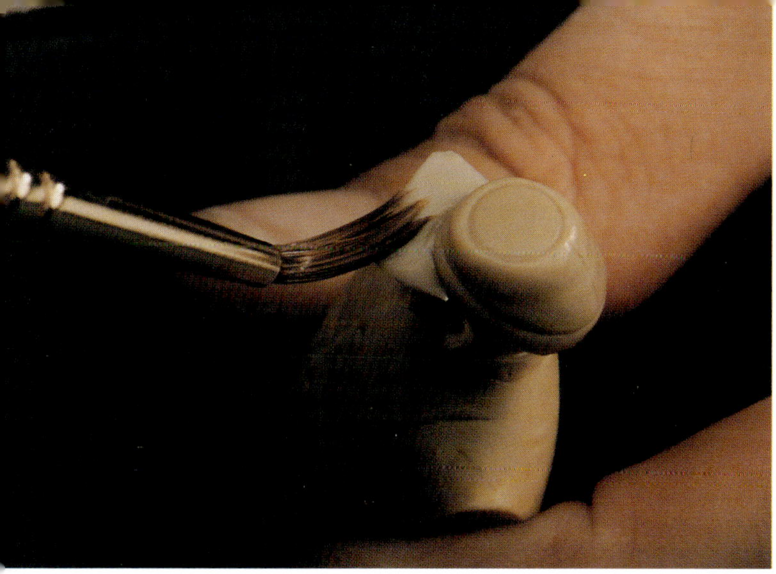

Smooth out the putty using a paint brush, dragging it toward the edges of the bill.

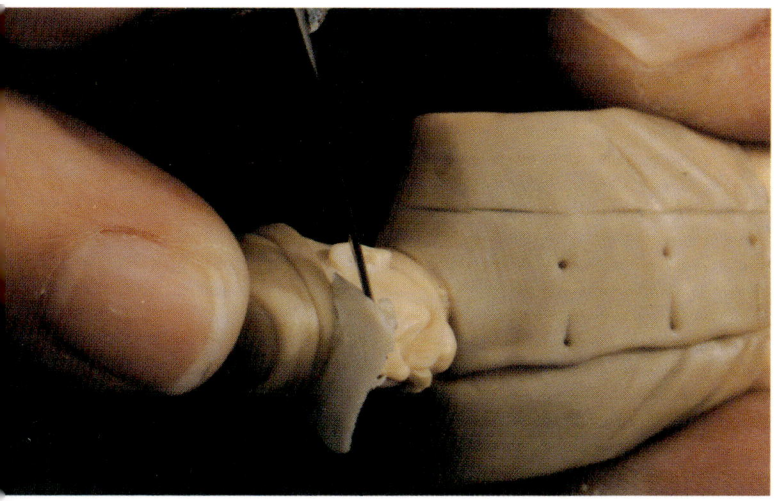

Trim away the excess putty with your X-acto knife.

The finished bill.

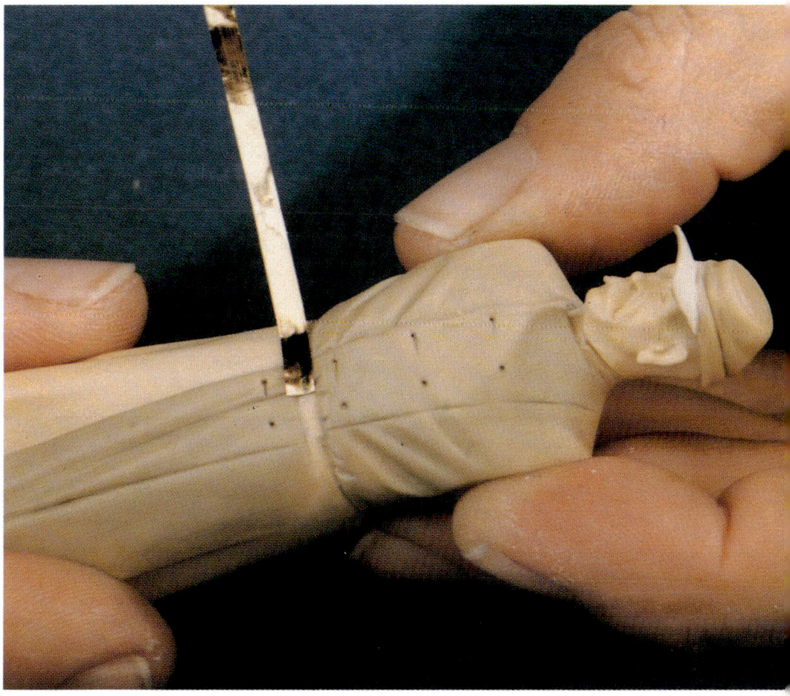

Next we'll construct the belt. For the belt material I use sections of old ointment tubes. It used to be that old toothpaste tubes were of the same material as old ointment tubes and if you can find them, they work great. Most of them however today are made out of plastic which will not work. Cut the tube open, clean out all of its contents with soap and water. Roll the tube out flat with your X-acto knife or a dowel rod and you're ready to cut belts. Start by placing the cut belt material at the front, where the buckle will be. A little dab of glue will help hold the end in place. Tack it with glue in three or four spots as you wrap the belt around the body.

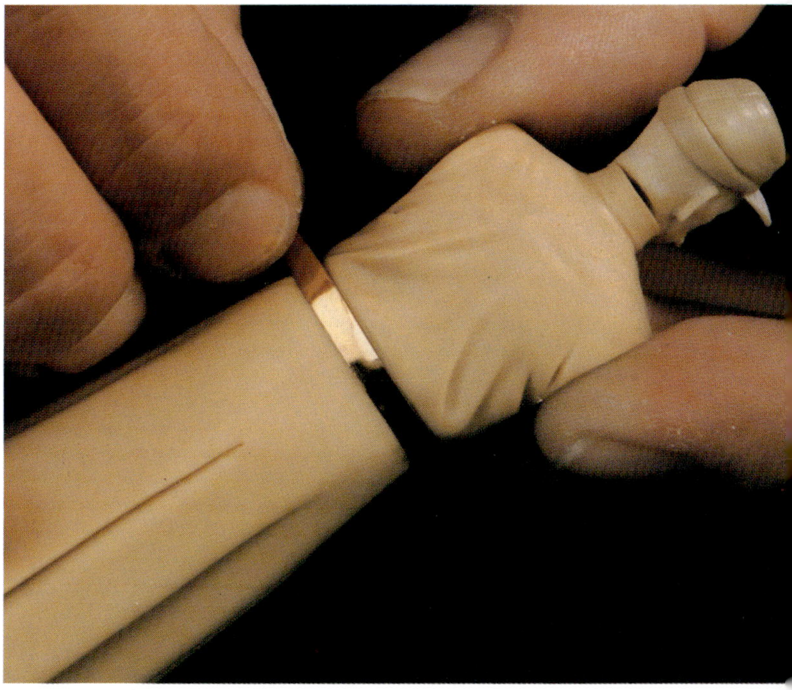

Wrapping the belt around the back.

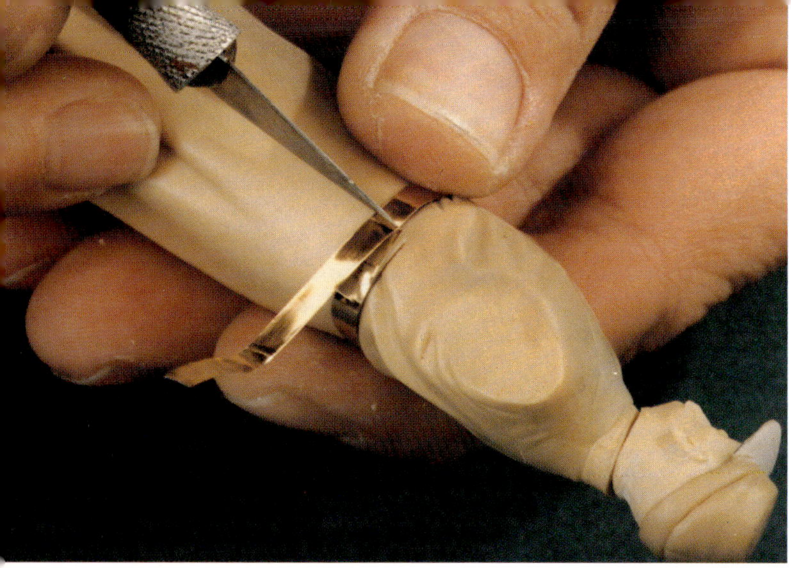

The first belt piece will wind up under the left arm. If our tube was long enough to get a single piece we would use only one piece. However, it wasn't and we will hide the splice beneath the left arm. With the second piece of belt, begin again at the buckle and end up under the left arm. Cut the excess belt material off with the X-acto knife.

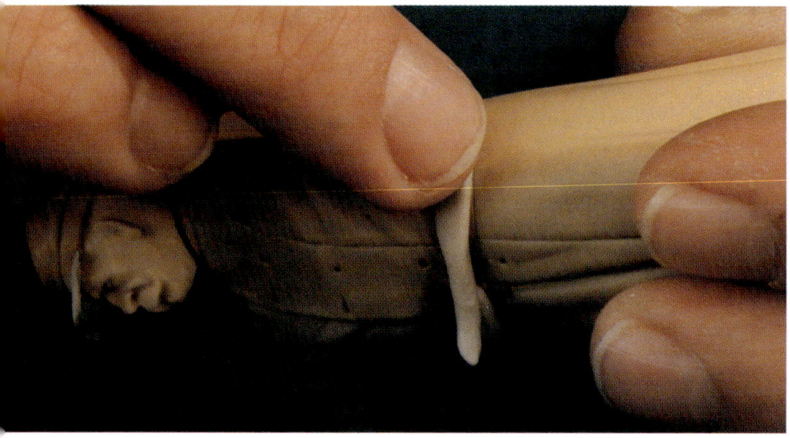

Roll out a thin snake of putty and apply it to the belt to give it some dimension. Press it in place with your finger.

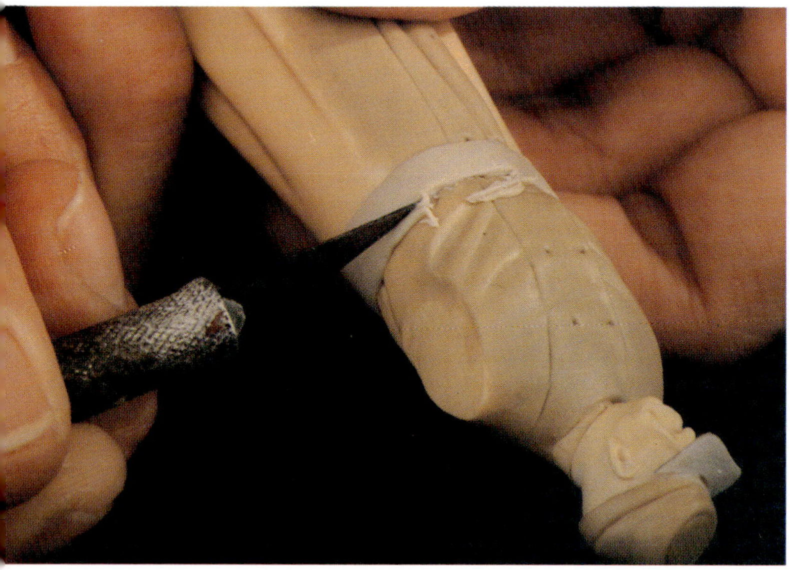

Smooth out the belt evenly around the figure and trim the belt to size.

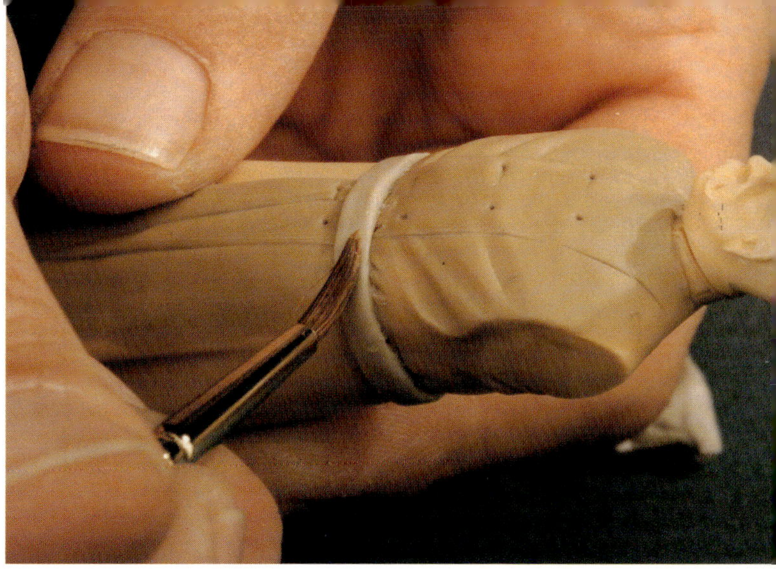

With a moistened brush, smooth out the belt, staying mainly toward the center of the belt to give it the characteristic cupped look of wider belts.

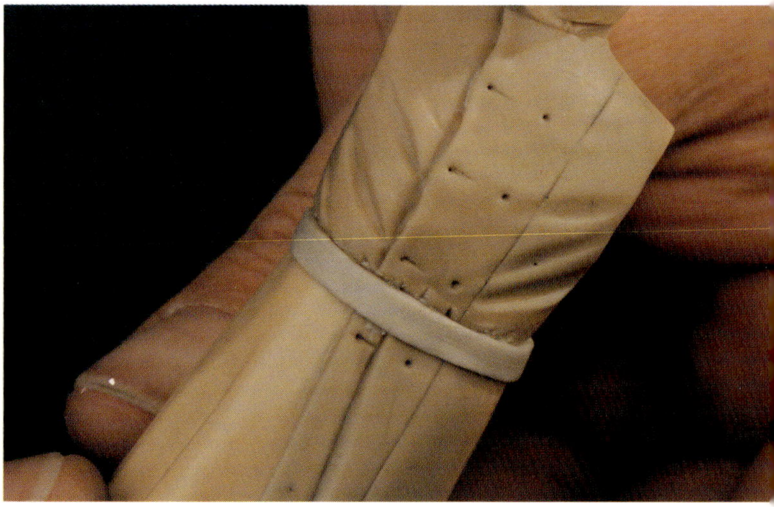

The completed belt. We will add the buckle and the holster support after we bake the belt.

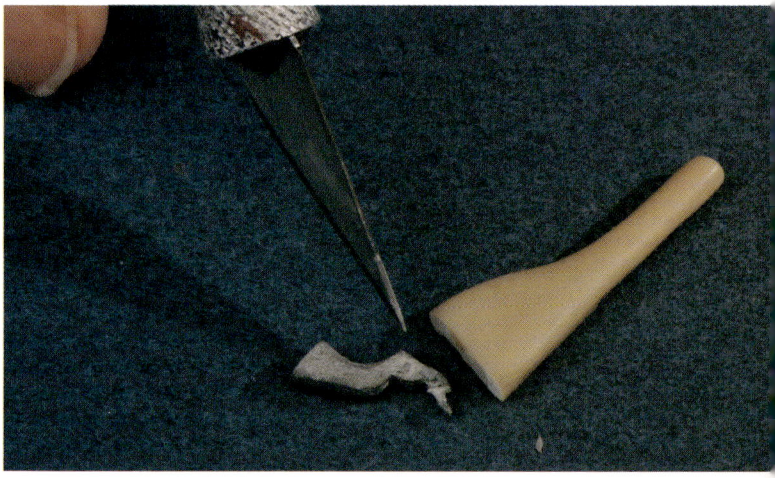

Now that the holster has baked, we can complete its shape, cutting off the points that we left when we cut it earlier. For the handle of the Colt 44 we have cut off the handle and hammer from a commercial casting that happens to be of the appropriate size.

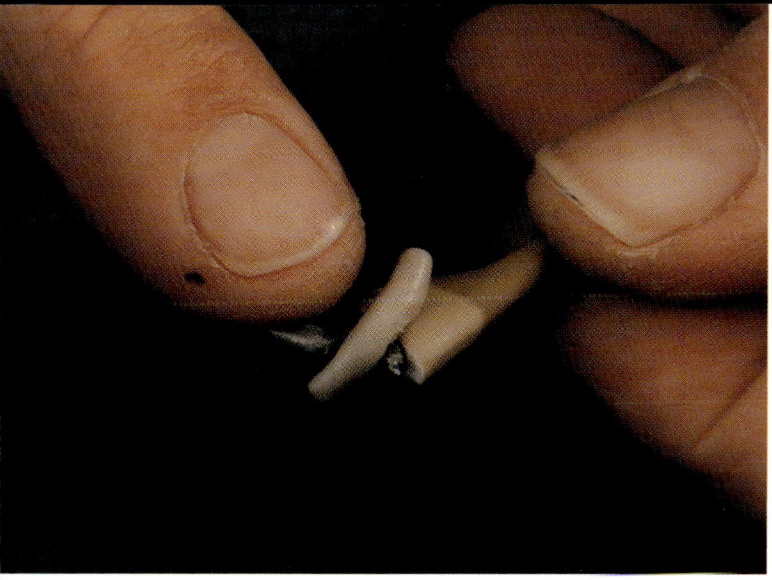

The butt is now glued onto the holster. Form the holster flap.

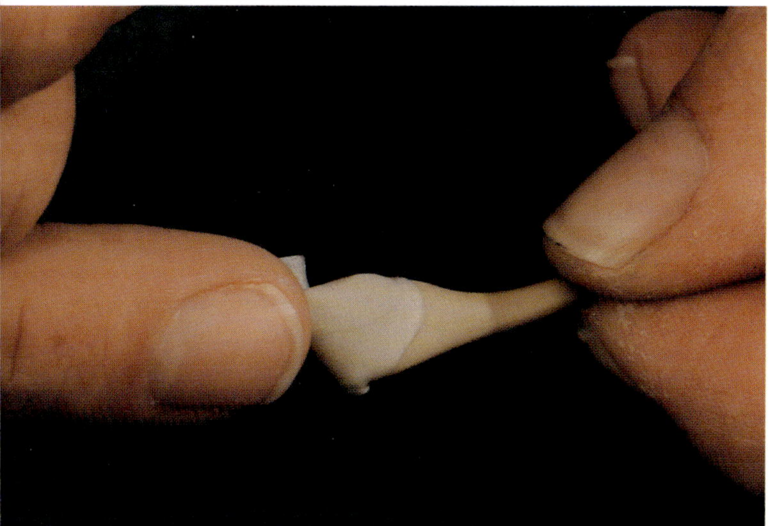

The initial shape of the holster flap.

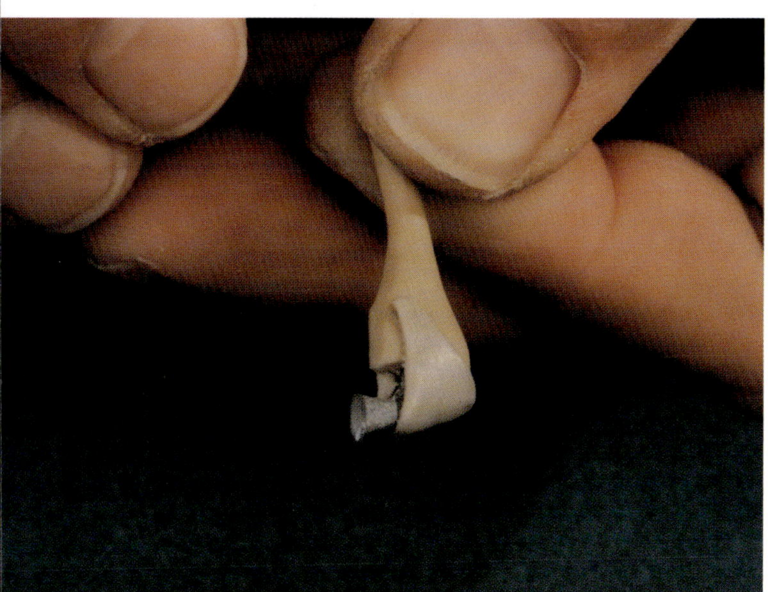

Trim the holster flap to shape with the X-acto knife.

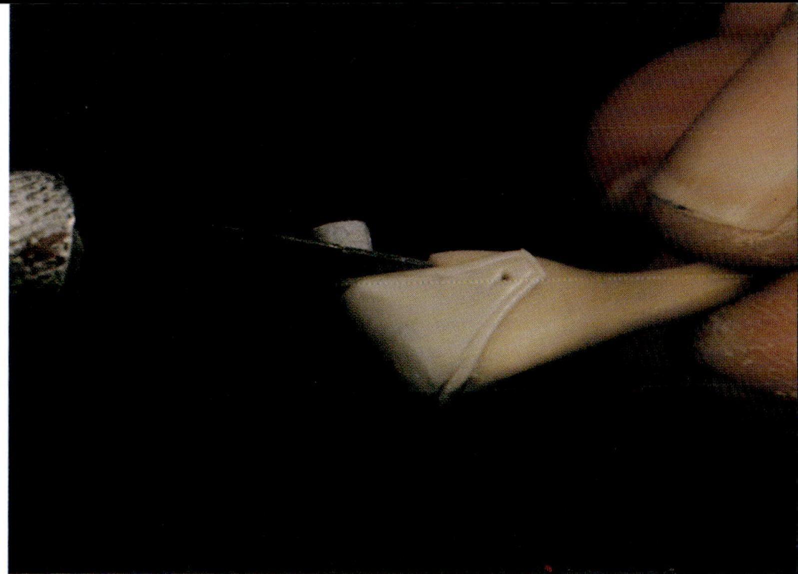

Adding details to the flap such as seams and the hold down stub. This holster is ready for the oven.

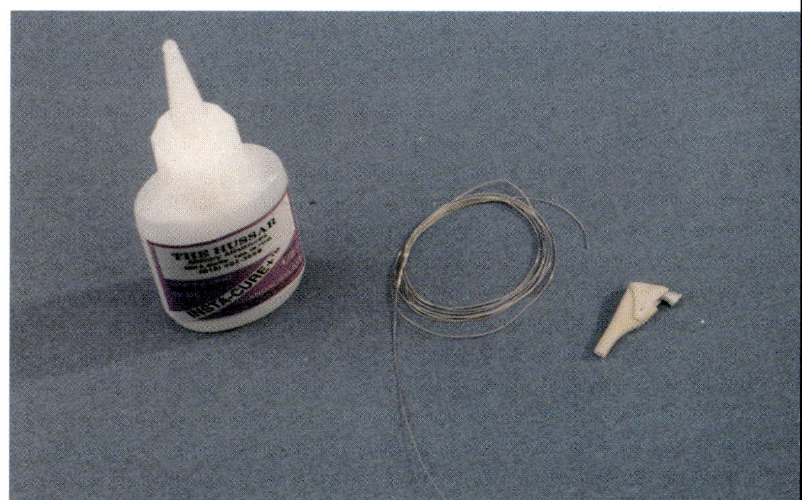

Using fine wire solder and Super Glue, we'll put a seam down the back side of the holster.

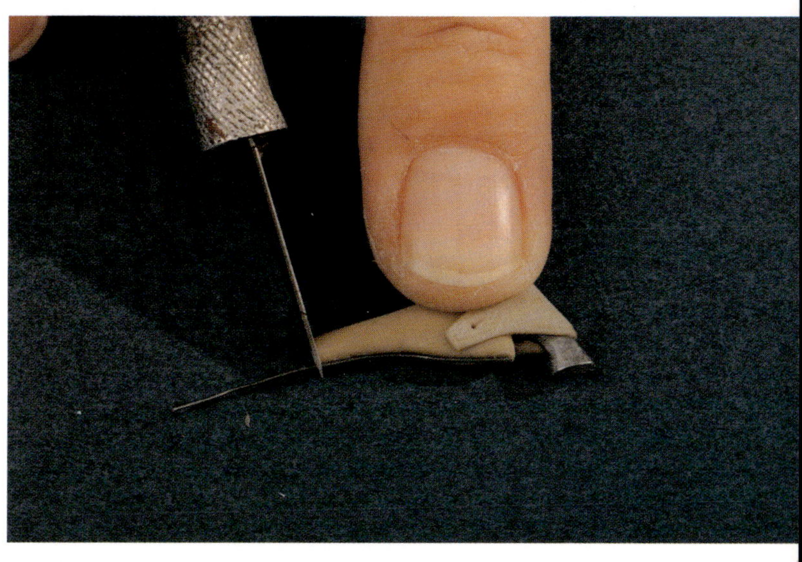

Apply glue to the solder. Apply the solder to the back edge of the holster and trim off the excess solder.

At this point we'll glue on the arms.

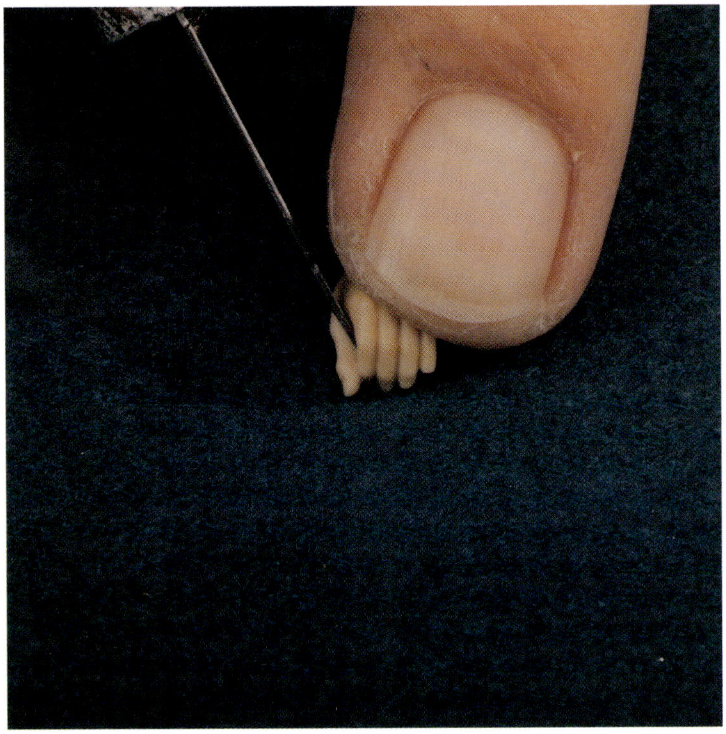

I wanted to tuck the thumb of the left hand underneath the belt, so I remove the kit's thumb from the left hand.

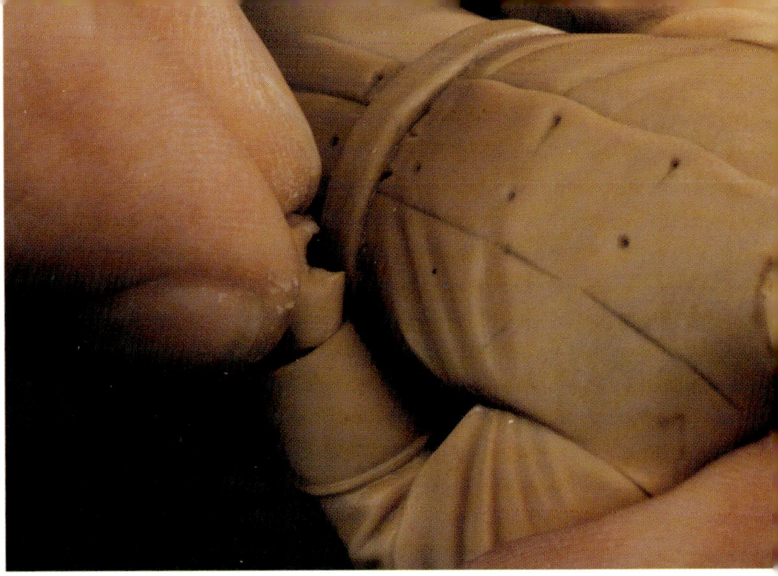

Glue the hand in place, positioned it over the belt.

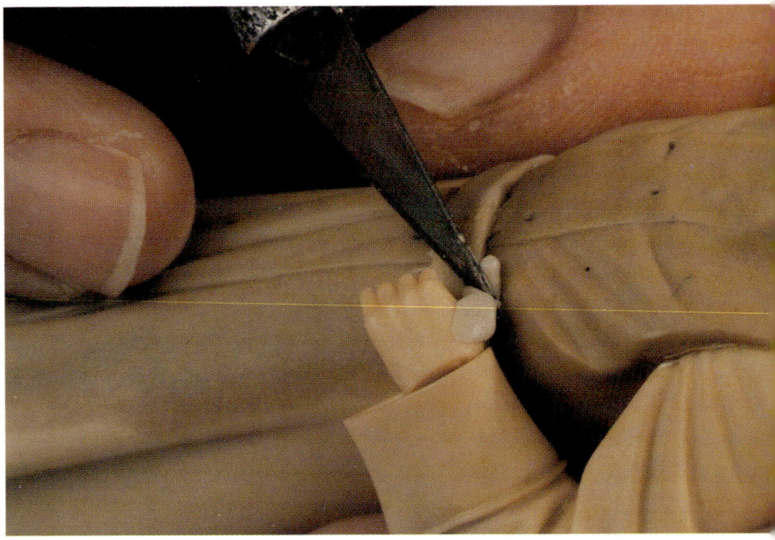

Apply a length of putty for the new thumb and remove the excess.

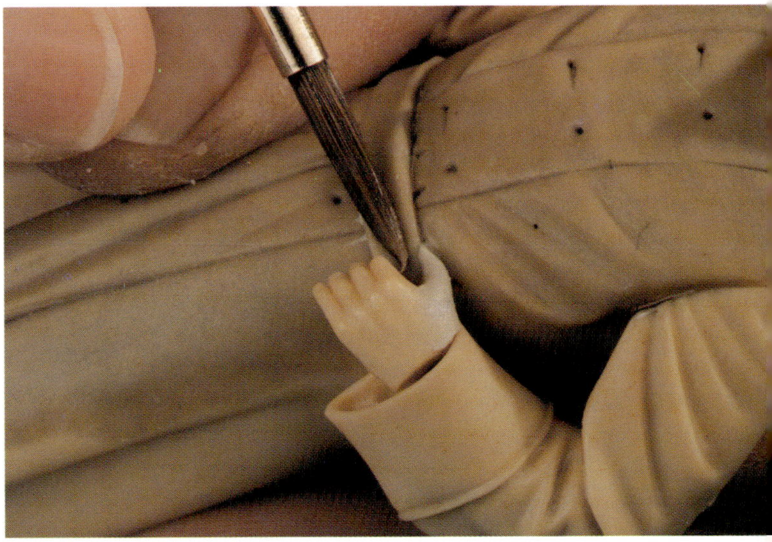

Forming the thumb with the point of a brush, giving it the appearance of being tucked in behind the top of the belt. Make sure that all of the transitions from resin to putty are smooth.

Fill in the seams between the hand and the arm with putty.

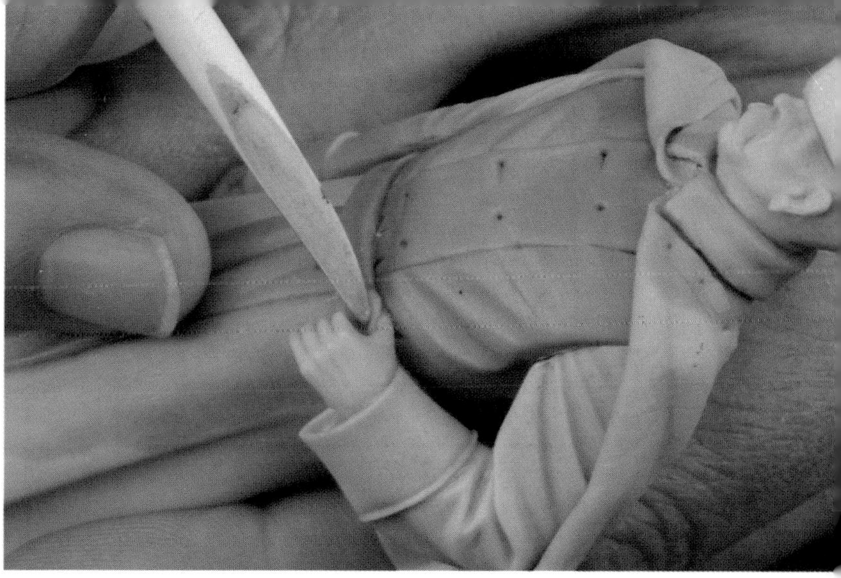

Apply a piece of putty to the belt where the thumb appears to extend beneath it. Work it in around the thumb.

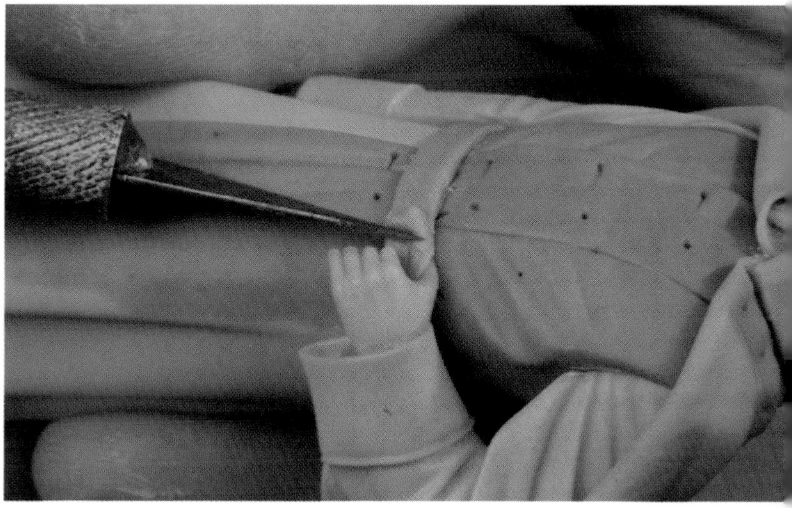

Trim off the excess.

The finished hand, ready for baking.

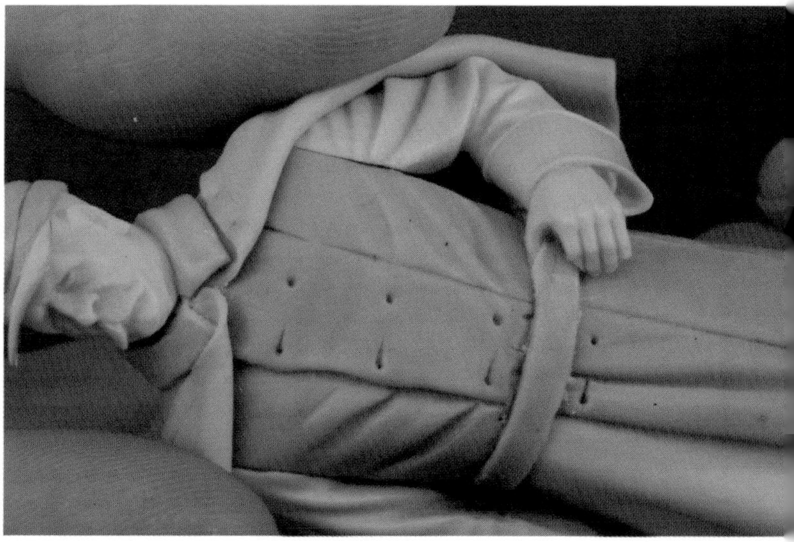

Then smooth the putty into the existing belt with a moistened brush so that we have a smooth transition between the two. Now it appears as if the soldiers thumb is pulling out the top of the belt from behind it.

Trim out the putty behind the belt so that it looks like it is actually pulling away from the body. Be careful that the belt does not get wider at that point.

The finished belt and thumb.

We'll begin to work on the cape of the coat. For that, we will need vegetable oil, a plastic sandwich bag, a ball of epoxy putty that is nearly too hard to work with, and a piece of dowel rod or something similar to roll the putty out. We use the vegetable oil to keep the putty from sticking to the inside of the bag when we roll it out. Some people prefer petroleum jelly but I find that the oil is easier to clean off.

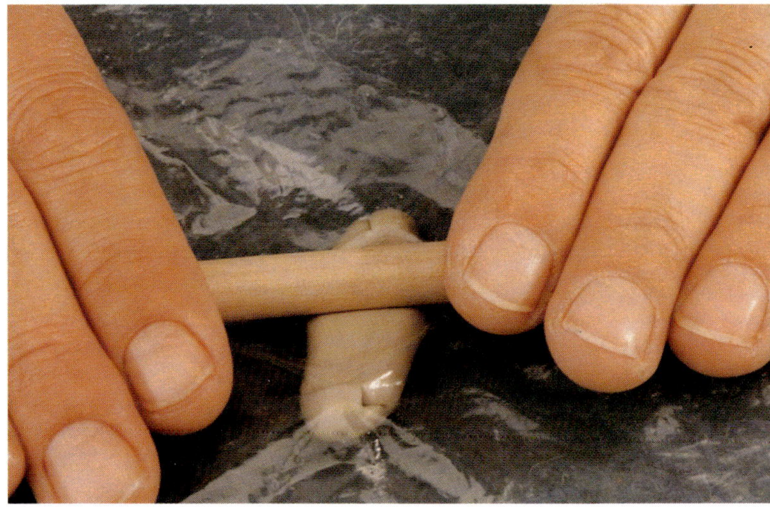

Lightly coat the inside of the sandwich bag with vegetable oil. Place the putty inside the oil coated bag, close the bag to keep the oil from leaking out, and then begin to roll the putty with the dowel rod as though you were rolling dough.

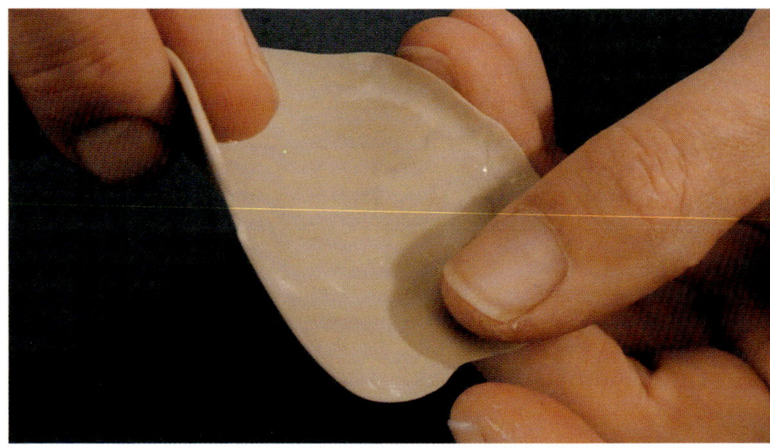

You want to roll the putty out as thin as possible without holes developing. If the putty is still thick, you can use it and thin down the edges after the cape has been applied. This technique is not only good for making capes on figures but is also an excellent way to make flags and standards. Note the flexibility and thinness of the putty when you are finished.

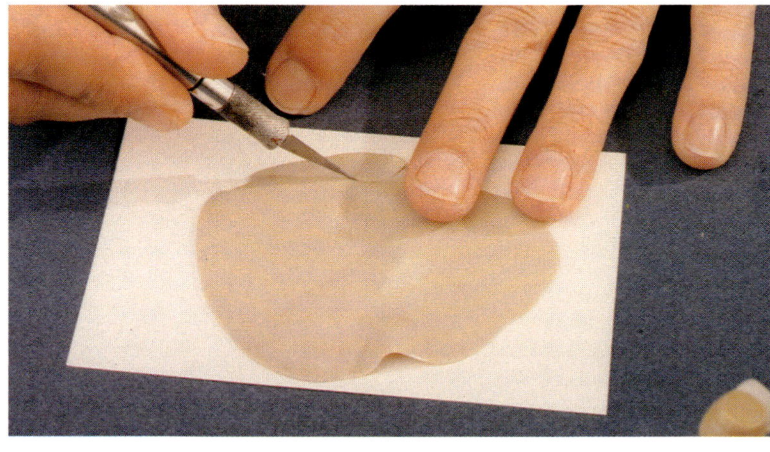

Cut out a semi-circular hole so that the cape will fit around the cavalryman's neck.

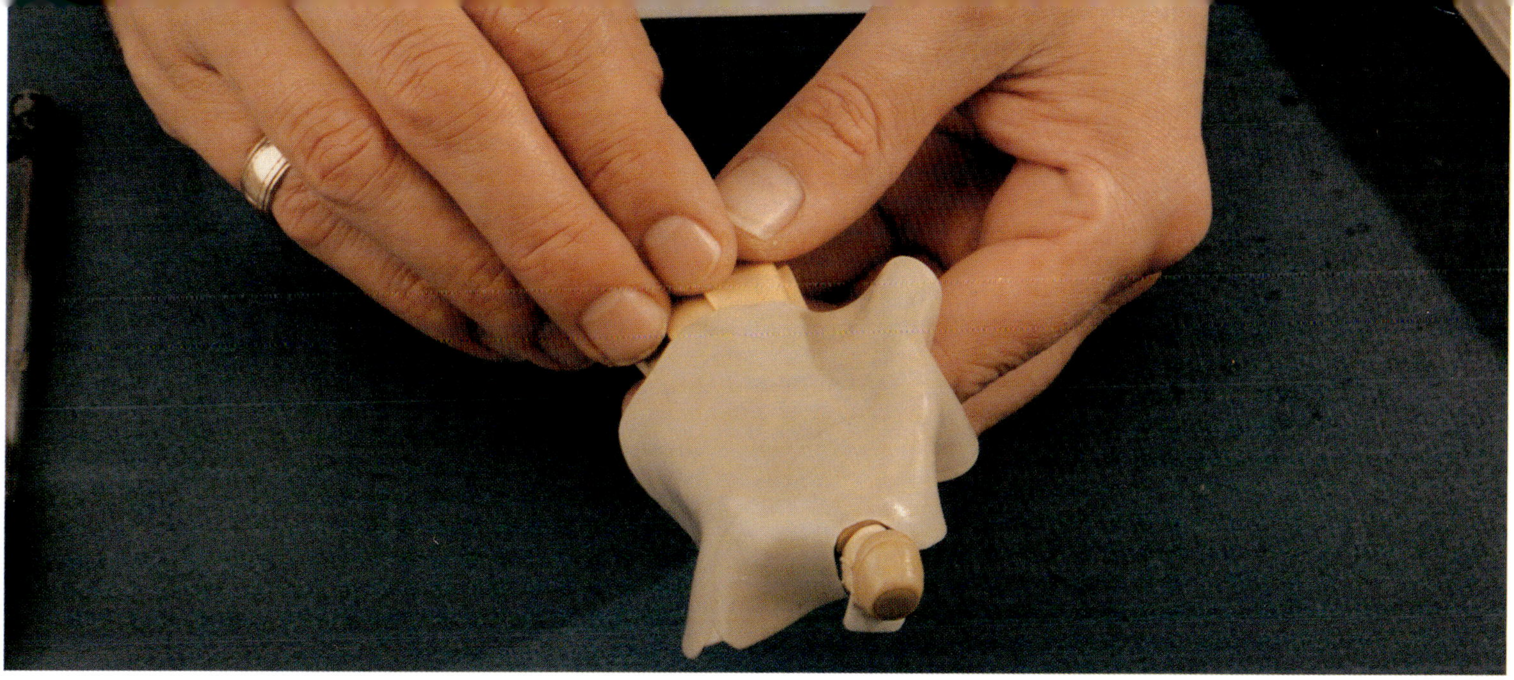

Drape the cape over the figure for sizing.

Bring the cape together under the chin, gently pulling on the putty to stretch it. Front and back view after draping the cape on the figure.

Trim the cape to size before adding folds and wrinkles.

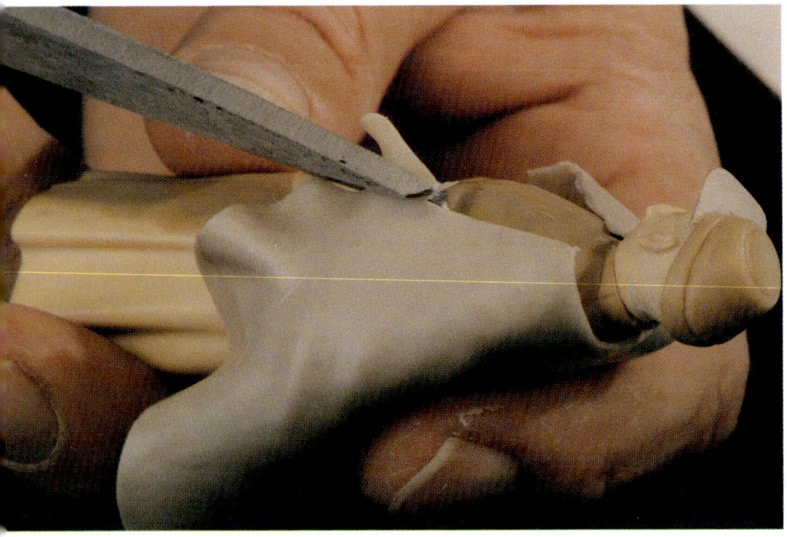

If trimming with the knife causes the cape to be misshapen, scissors may be better.

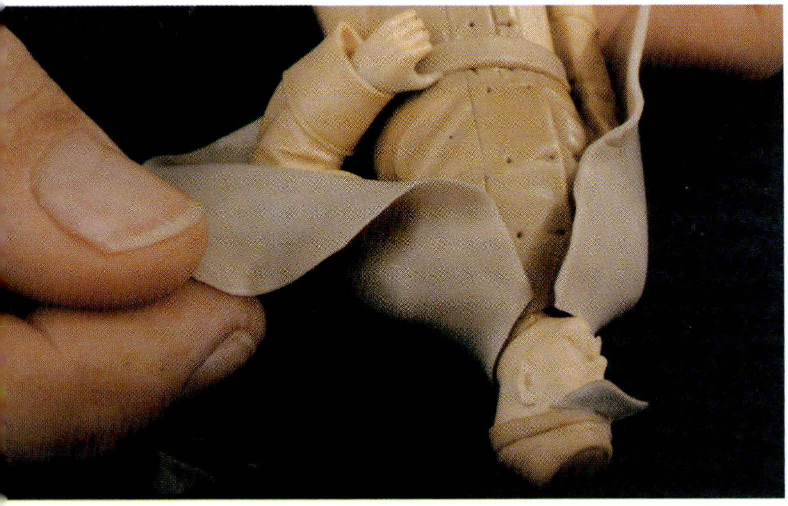

Gently turn back the flap of the cape on both sides. If you have trouble keeping the collar closed under the chin, it is okay to glue it in place at this time.

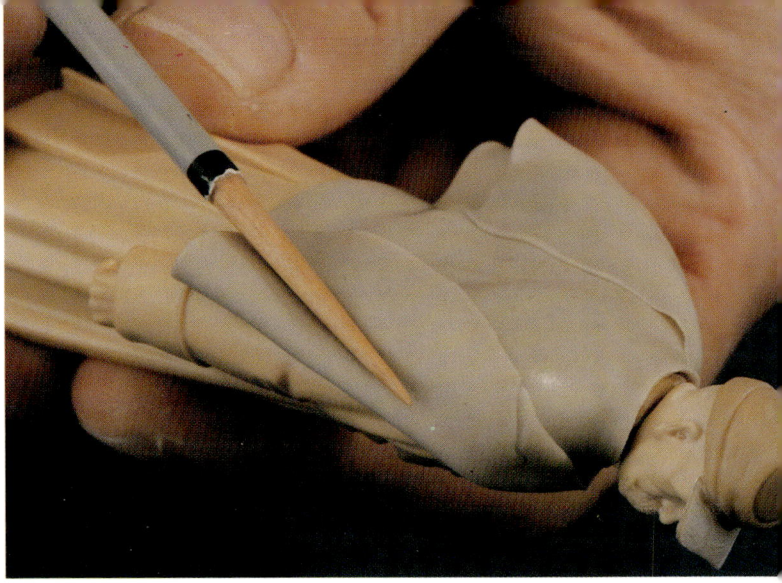

While gently turning back the edges of the cape, be careful to make the folds and wrinkles look convincing. While it is difficult at this stage to add folds and wrinkles, with persistence and pressure you can put in a few to make the drapery look convincing.

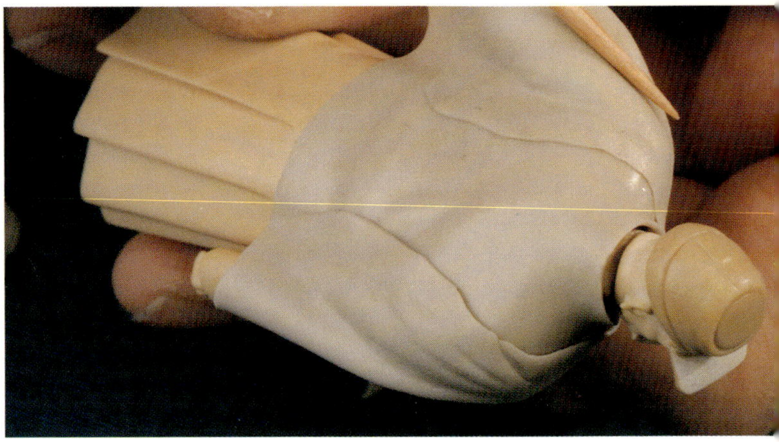

Wrinkles in place along one side of the cape.

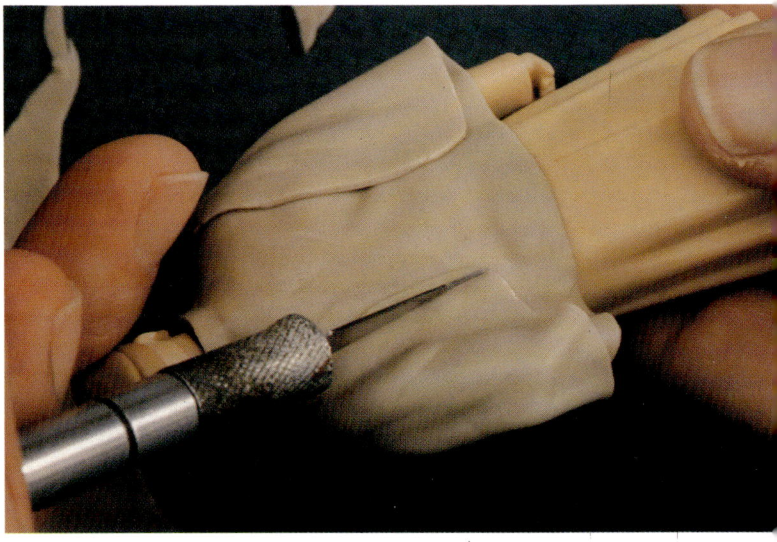

Add seam lines to the cape with an X-acto knife. Be careful not to remove the shape you have just put into the cape. If you wish, you can add the seam lines with paint later.

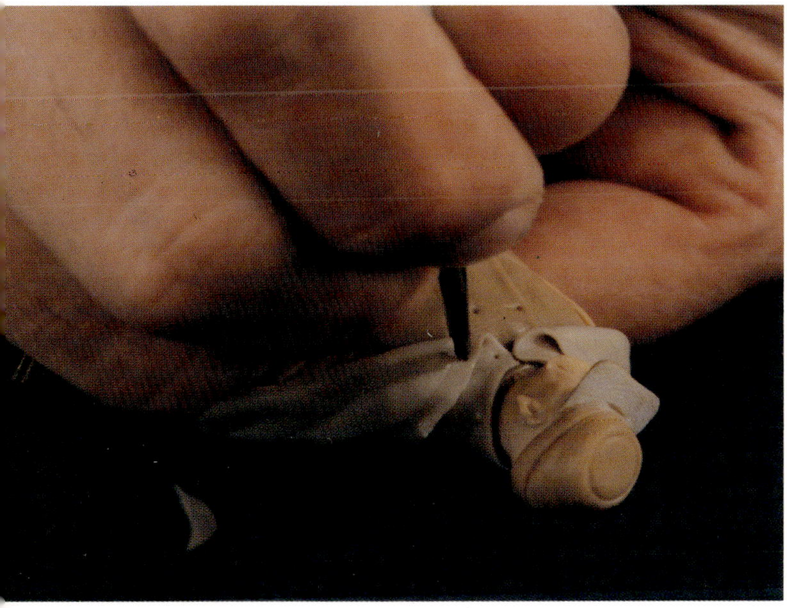

Take a straight pin and push it blunt end first into the handle of a paint brush. Use this new tool to add button holes to the cape.

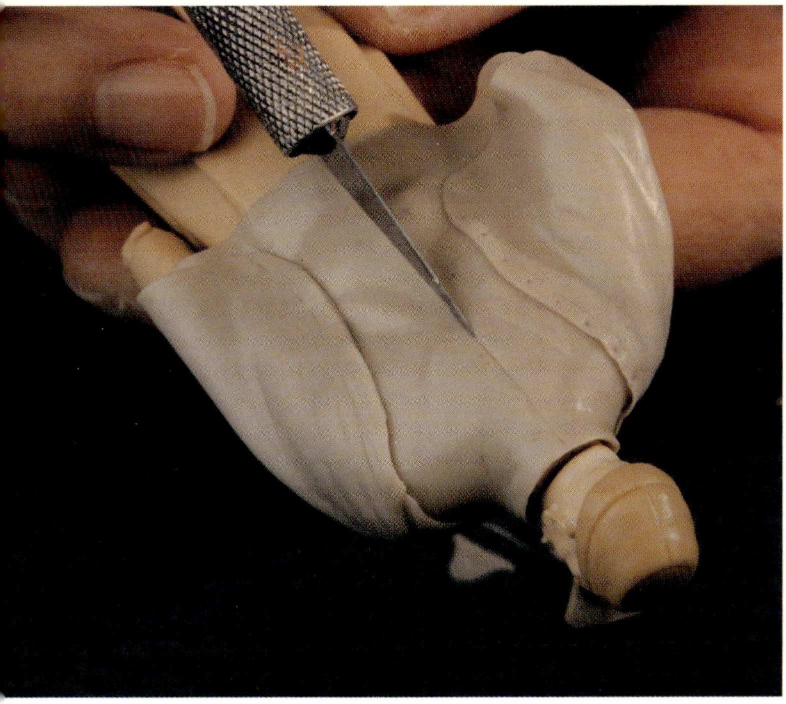

Use an X-acto knife to create a seam down the center of the back of the cape. Put in the oven in an upright position. As the heat softens the putty somewhat, it can sag and if it is in the upright position it will sag naturally. If you have trouble adding these details to the softened putty, they can be added after the putty has hardened by drilling in the button holes and scribing seam lines with a sharp X-acto knife.

The finished cape.

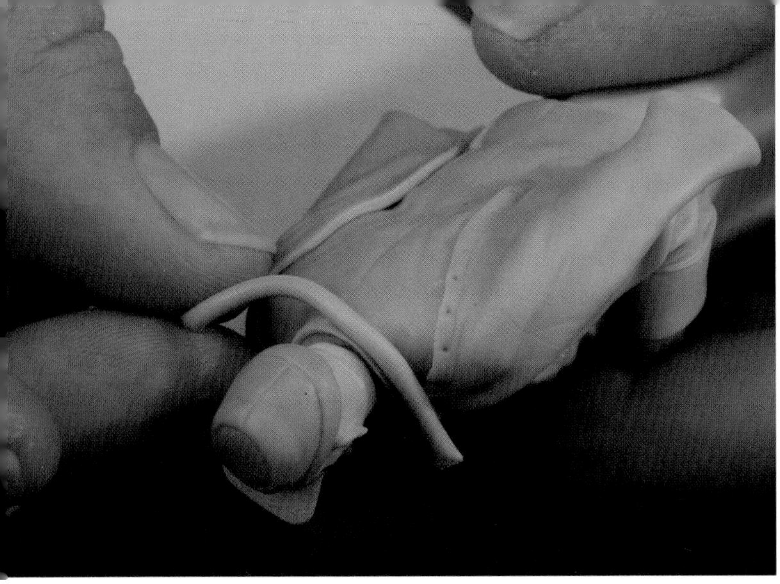

Add a roll of putty to make the collar.

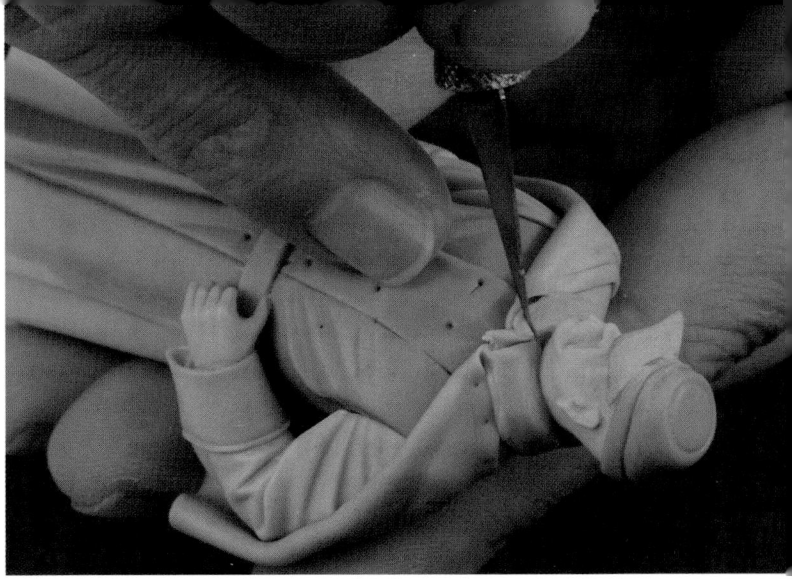

Cutting the collar to shape.

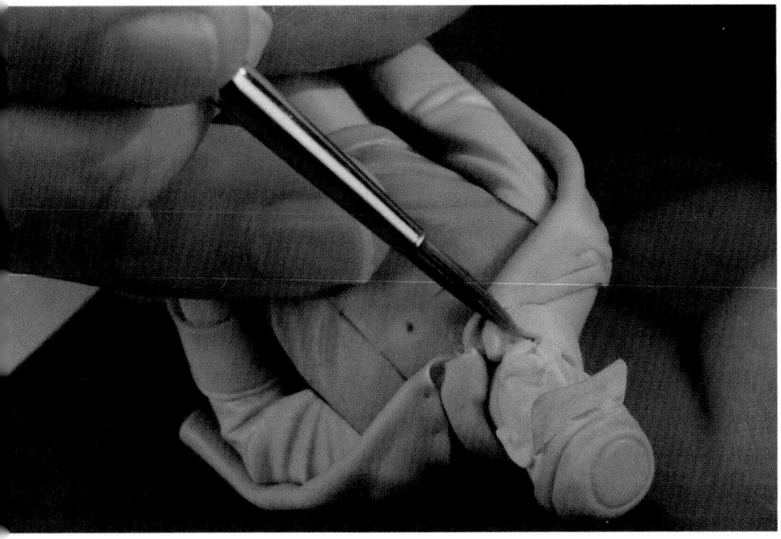

Flatten out the collar with your finger. Smooth out the collar with a moistened brush. Concentrate near the center of the collar as we did on the belt to create a cupping effect.

The finished collar.

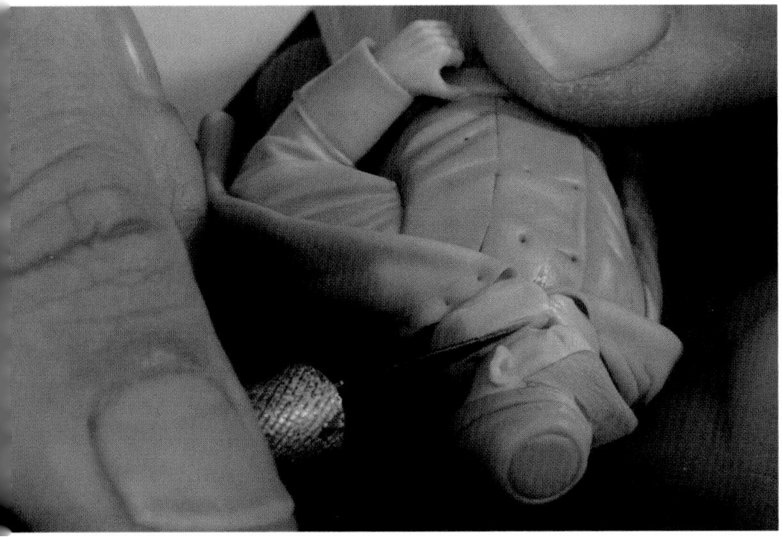

Shaping the outline of the collar and trimming away the excess.

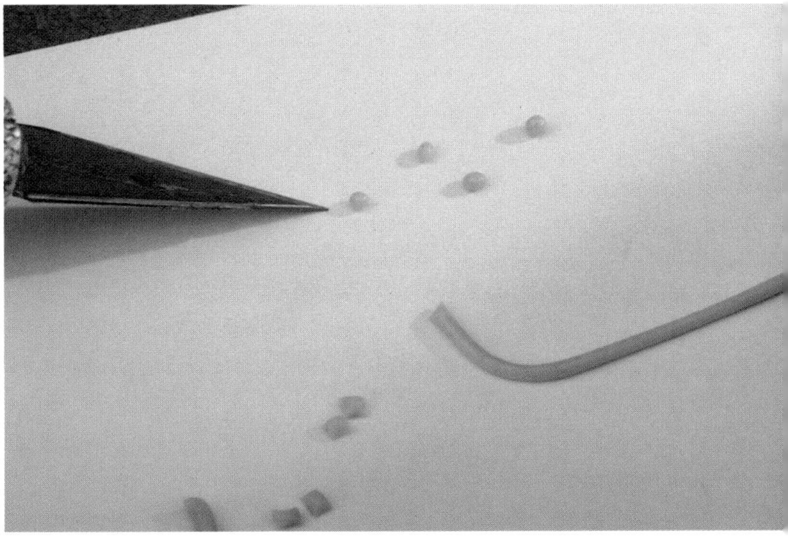

Roll out a thin snake of putty and cut small pieces off for buttons. This technique maintains the uniformity of size of each of the buttons. Roll the small sections that you have cut off into small balls.

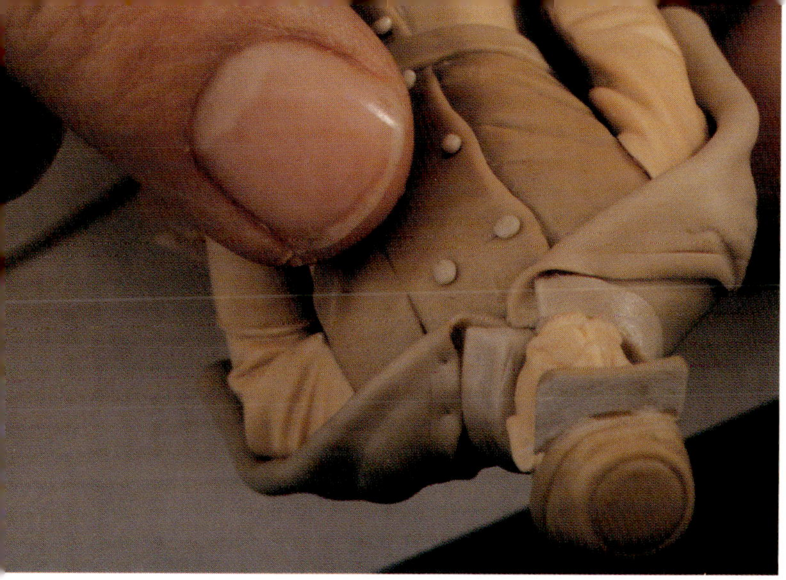

Pick the balls of putty up on the end of your finger. Place them in position over the button holes you made in the jacket earlier. With a moistened finger, gently press the buttons into place, trying to not flatten them too much because they are actually domed buttons.

Using another home-made tool (a paint brush with the hairs removed and the ferrule of the brush drilled out), we will push it over the buttons gently to create the rim around the buttons. Be careful not to push too hard or it will cut the buttons like a cookie cutter.

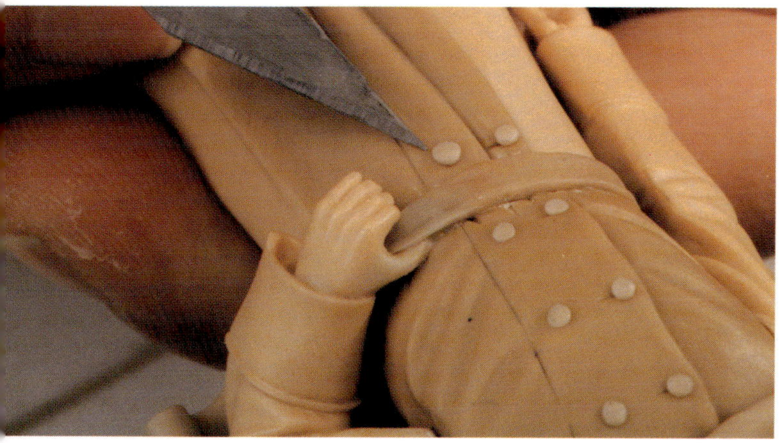

Check for uniformity. The button I am pointing to with the X-acto knife is too large. We will trim it down a bit and reshape it with a moistened brush.

The "uniform" buttons.

The completed buttons. Now to the oven.

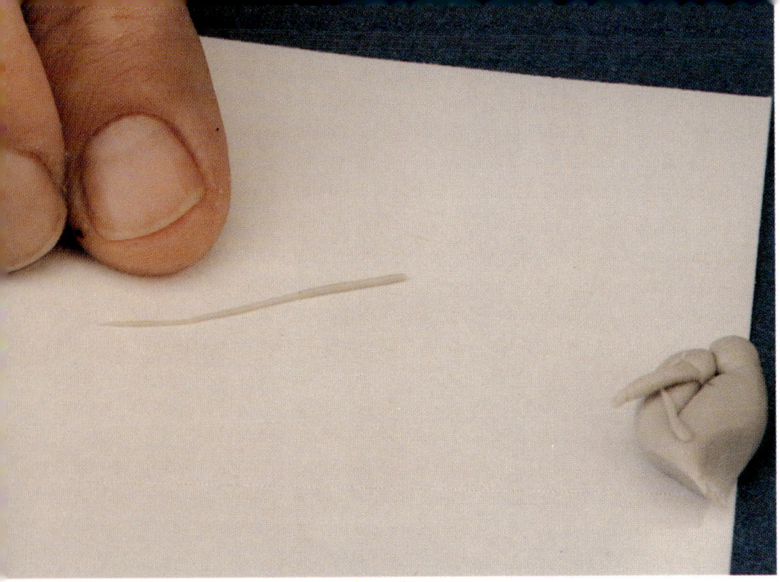

The beginnings of the crossed saber cap device. Roll out a very fine length of putty.

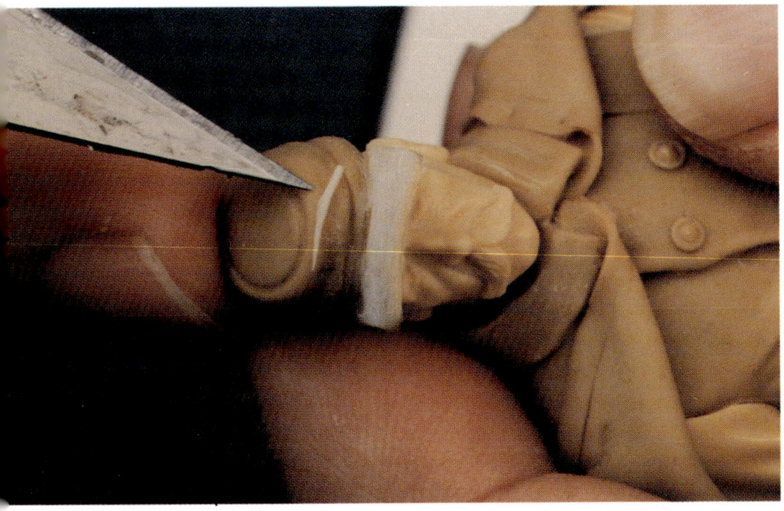

Apply the small length of putty on the front of the cap to begin the cap device. Pieces this small are best worked only with a moistened brush.

The crossed sabers placed on the kepi front before detailing.

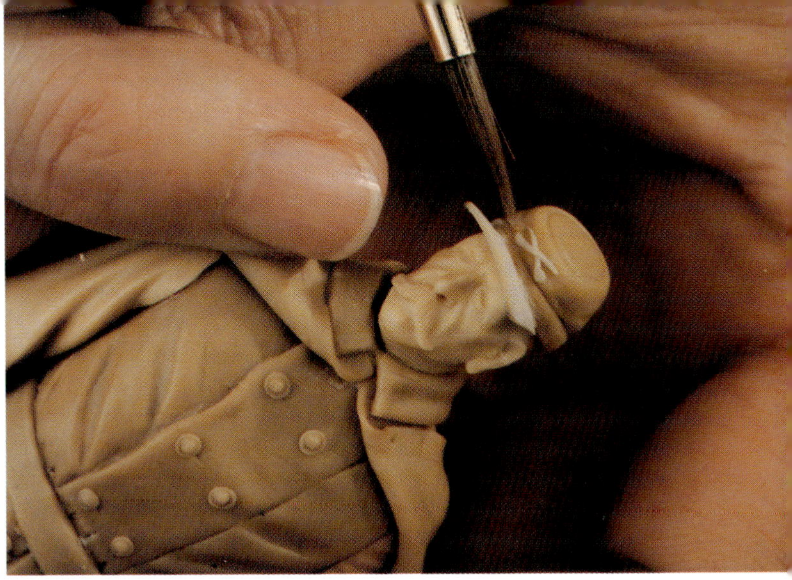

Shaping the hilt end of the crossed sabers with the brush.

The completed crossed sabers. Before we dry this in the oven we can drop down and put the belt buckle and holster suspender in place.

Apply putty for the belt buckle and trim it to size. We may have to trim again after we have done the detail work.

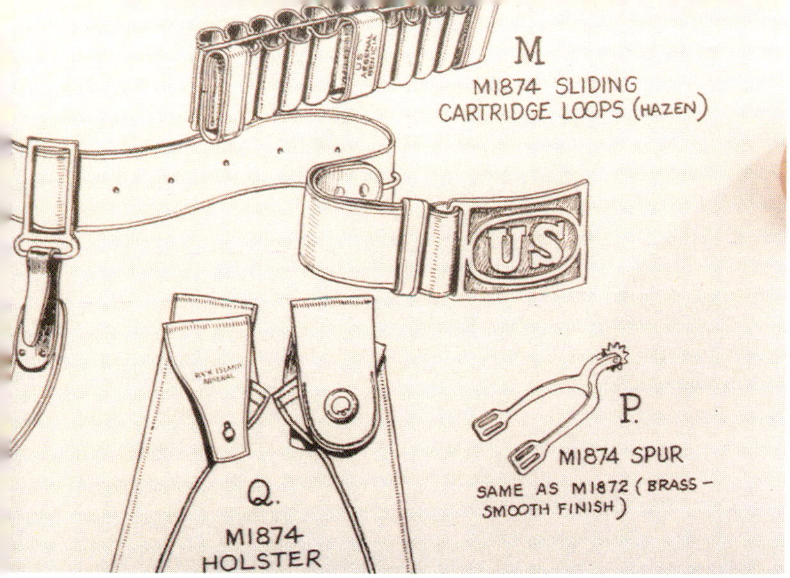

This is the belt buckle that we are modelling.

The oval around the US is taking shape.

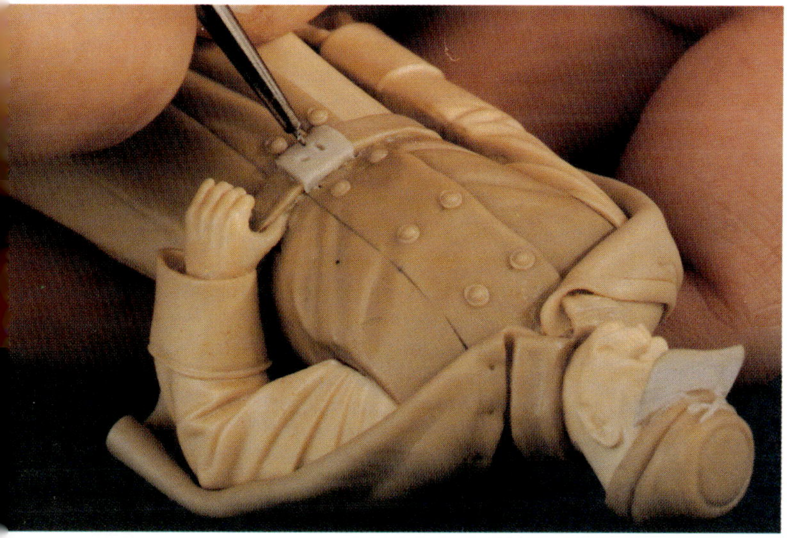

Starting from the center of the belt buckle, I simply use my straight pin tool and push down the putty in the areas I do not want raised.

While the belt buckle will eventually be rectangular, I'm cutting off the excess putty outside of the oval. I will bake it and then come back in and add the square corners. If we were to keep working on it from this point the rectangle would become misshapen and would not have square corners.

The US insignia begins to take shape.

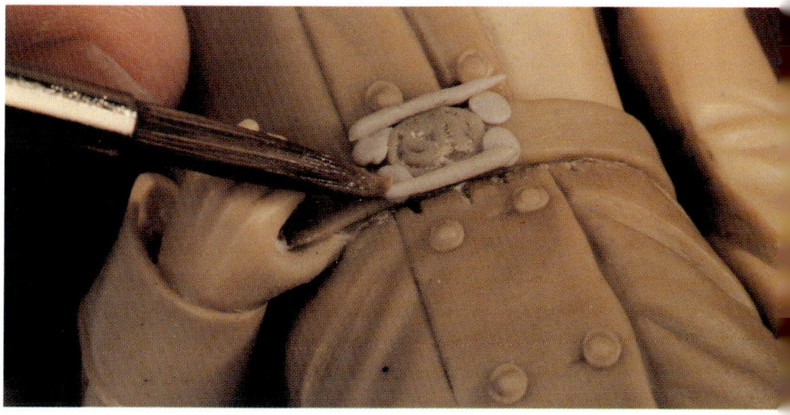

We will now add the corners to the belt buckle. Add four small flattened balls of putty at the corners and an outside edge to the belt buckle which will be trimmed down later.

Outlining the belt buckle.

Then cut to shape and trimming the slide loop up to its final shape.

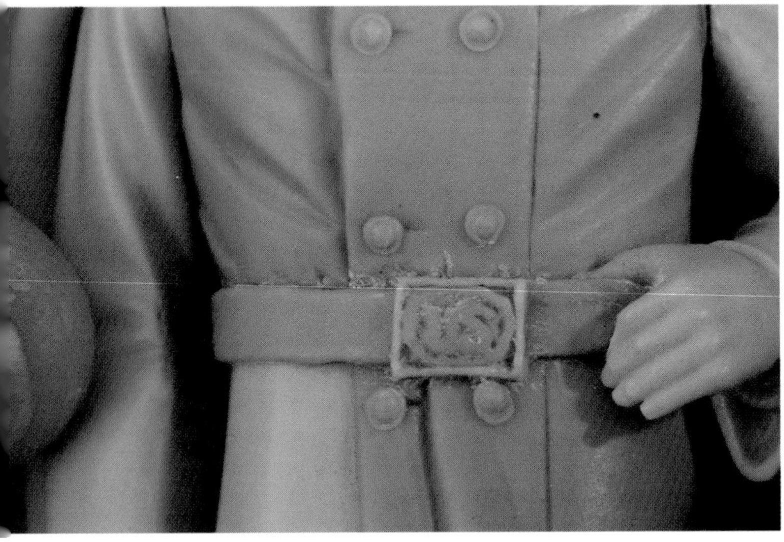

The finished belt buckle after trimming the sides.

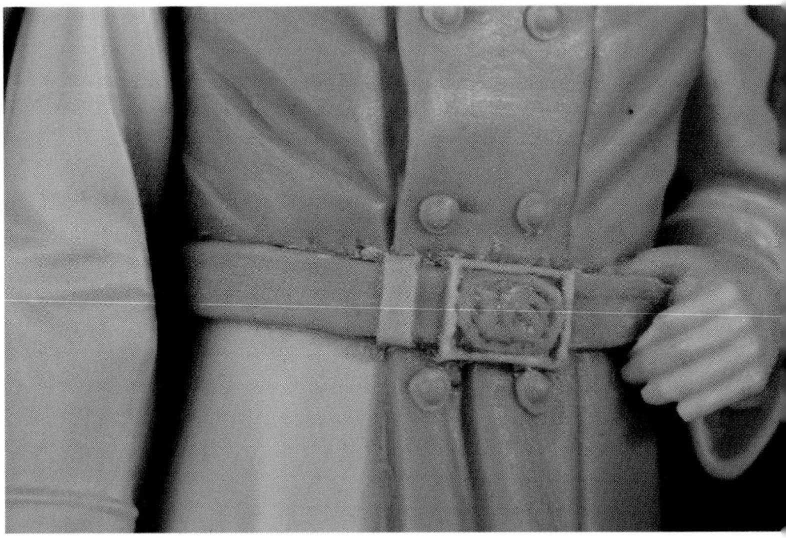

The finished belt loop.

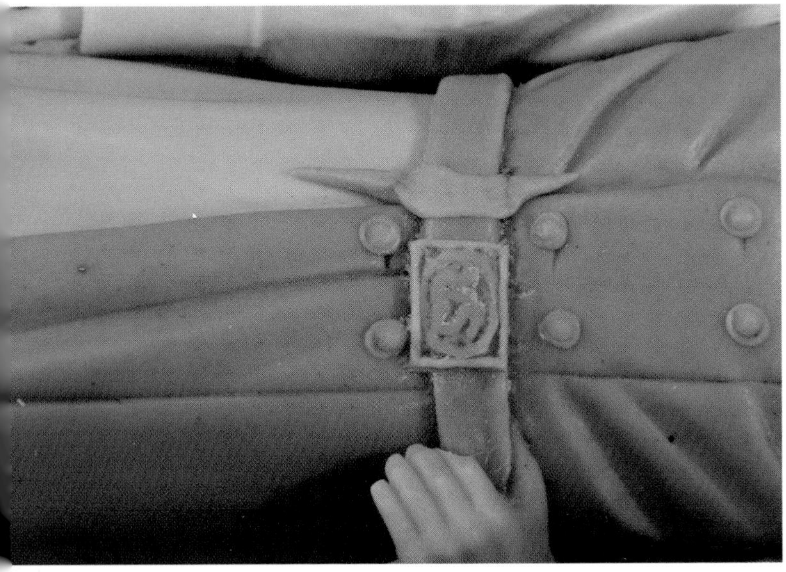

The beginning of the slide loop. Flatten the putty out with the paddle tool.

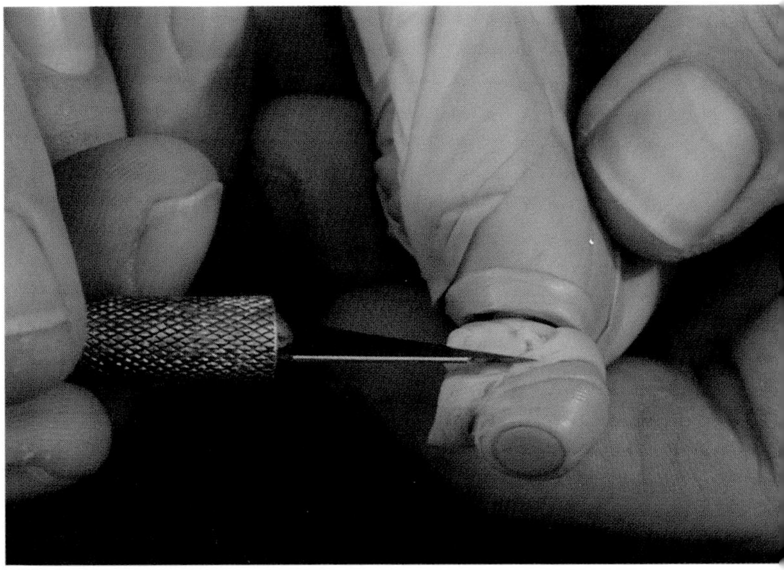

Place a roll of putty on the back of the head to begin to add hair to the figure. Work the hair forward toward the temples.

The putty for the hair laid in, ready for texturing.

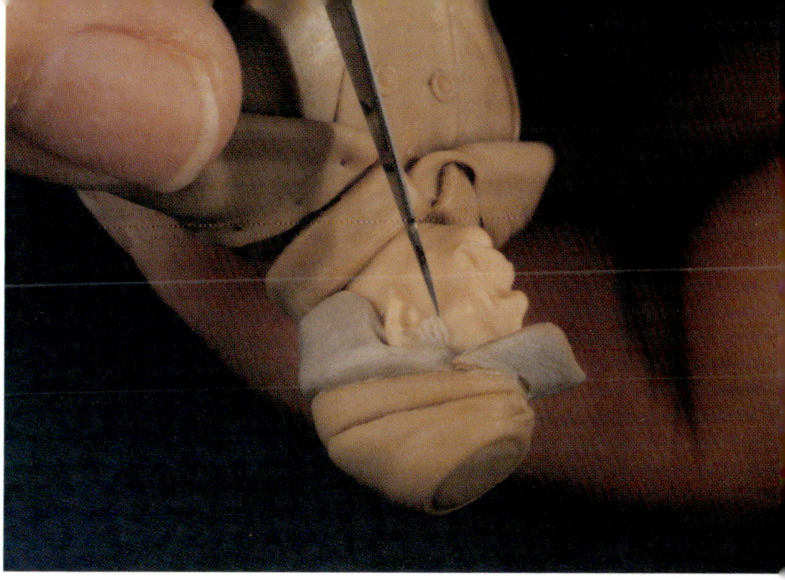

Texture the sideburns with a stippling motion.

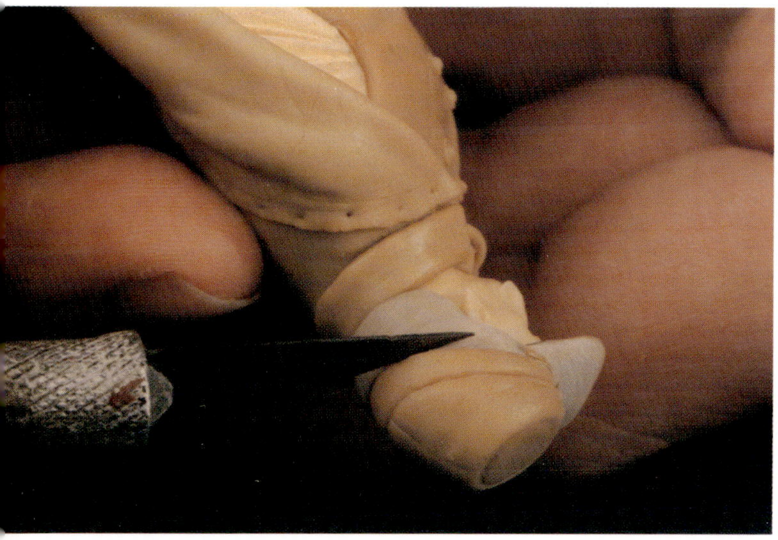

Begin by deliniating the bottom of the cap again.

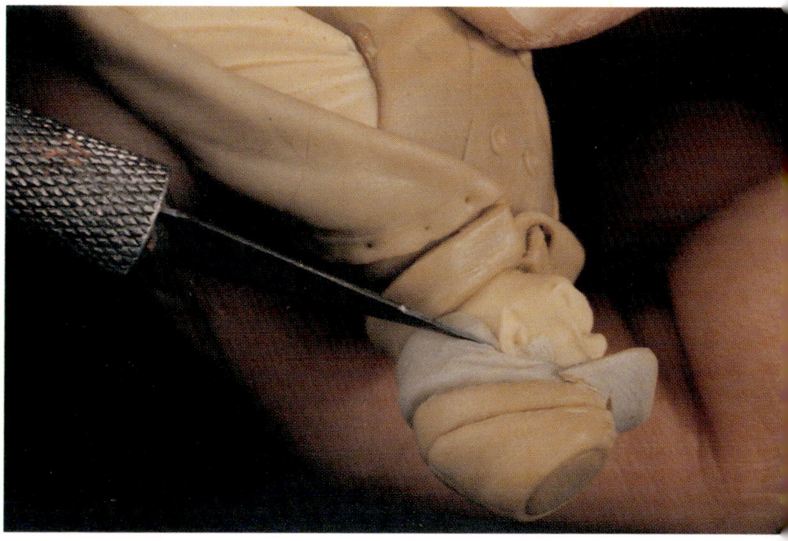

Texture the hair with lines following the contours of the head.

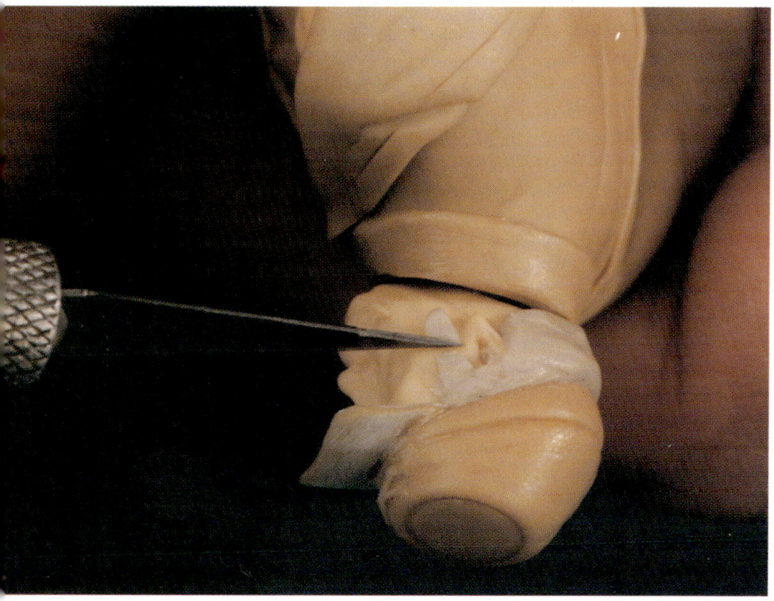

Applying and trimming sideburns.

The initial texturing.

The final texturing of the hair.

The cap band in place.

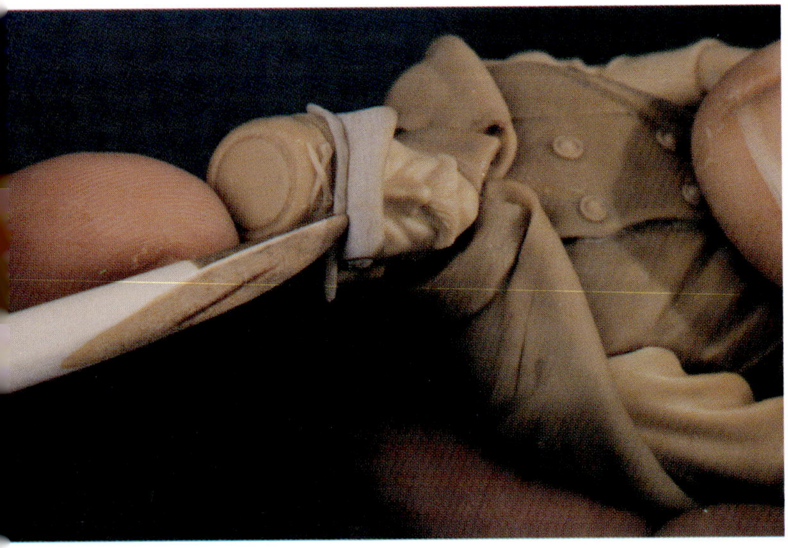

Add the cap band and press it into place.

Apply the holster strap to the belt.

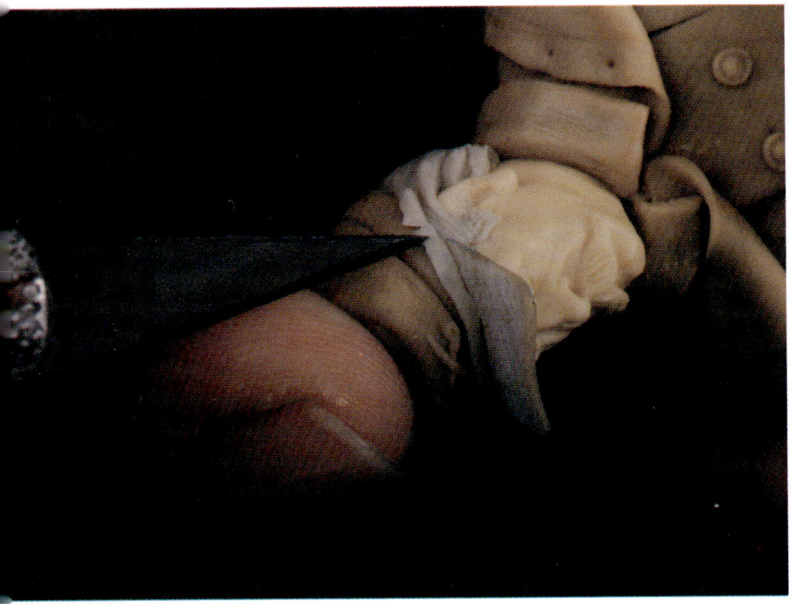

Trim the cap band to size.

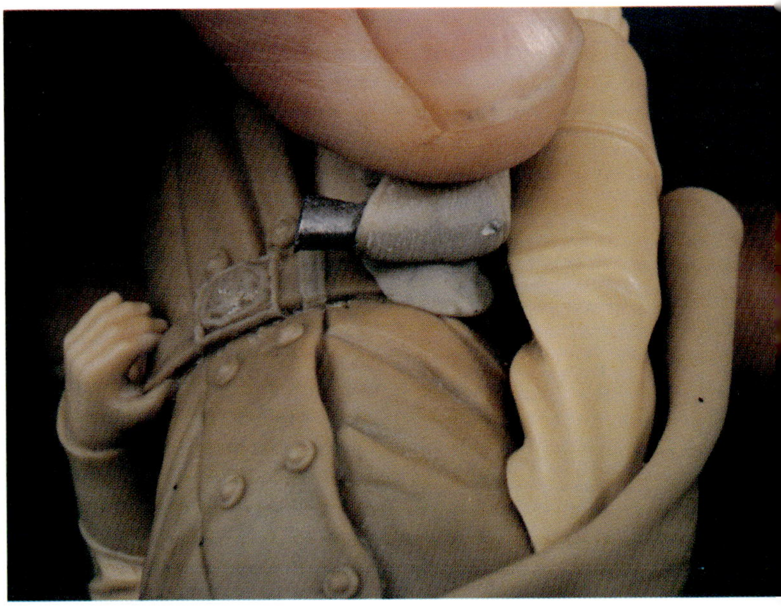

Press the holster into the wet putty to create a cavity.

The finished pistol holster strap.

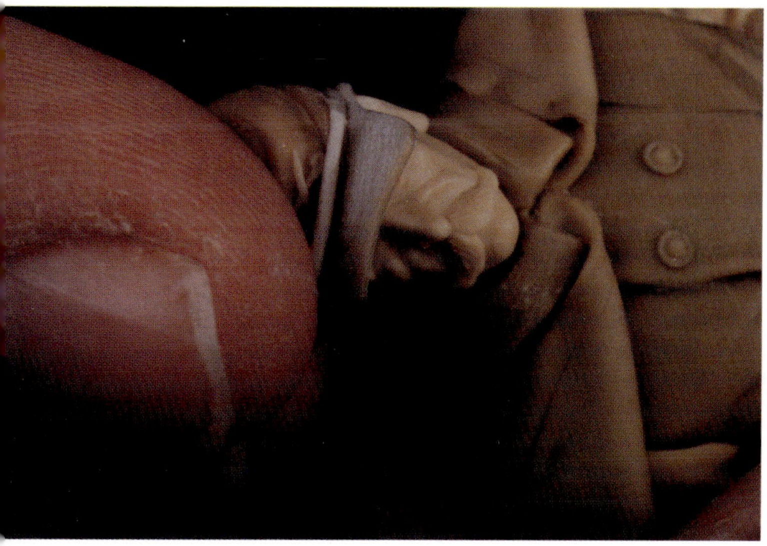

Adding details of the cap band. Apply a second, thin roll of putty to the right half of the band. Trim it into position, ending where it will meet the cap band buckle.

Smoothing the putty.

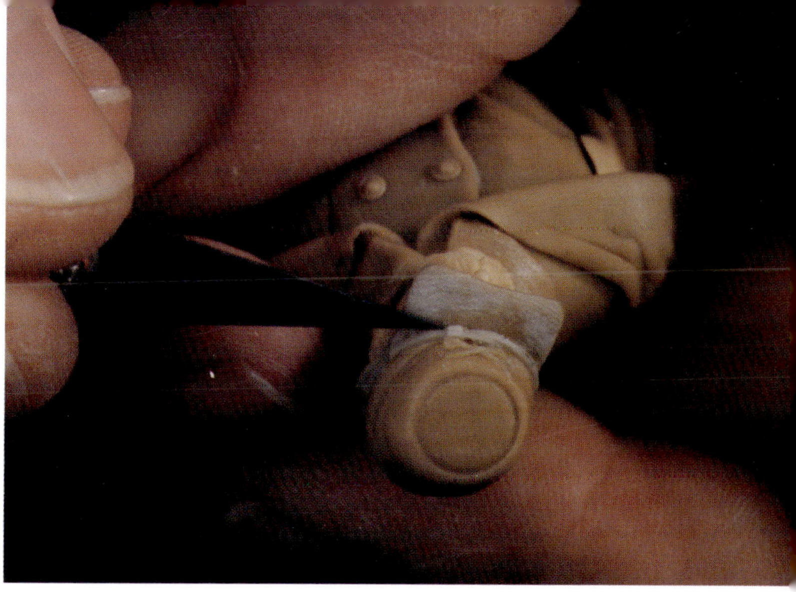

Add a ball of putty to form the buckle. Flatten the ball with a brush and trim to size.

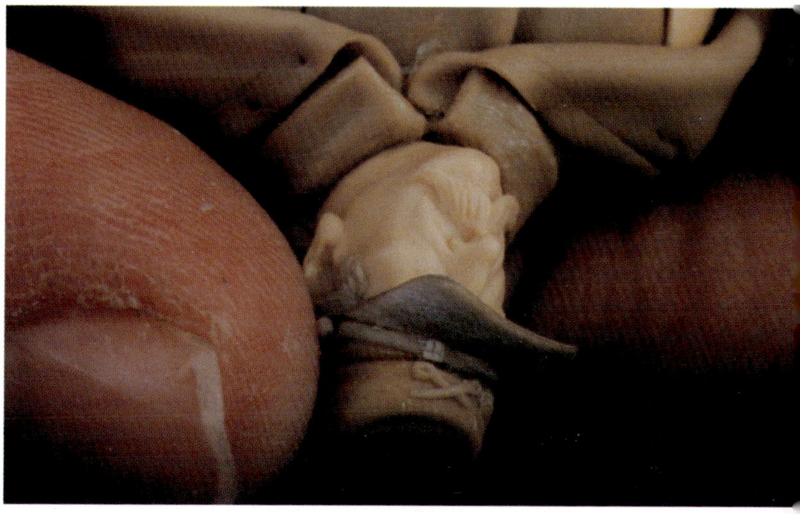

Add a button at either end of the cap band.

The cap details in place.

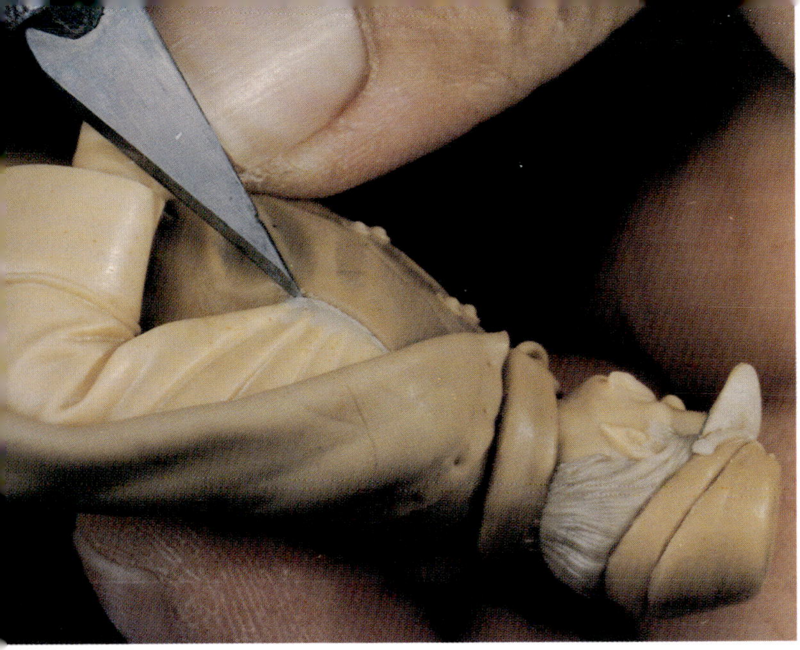

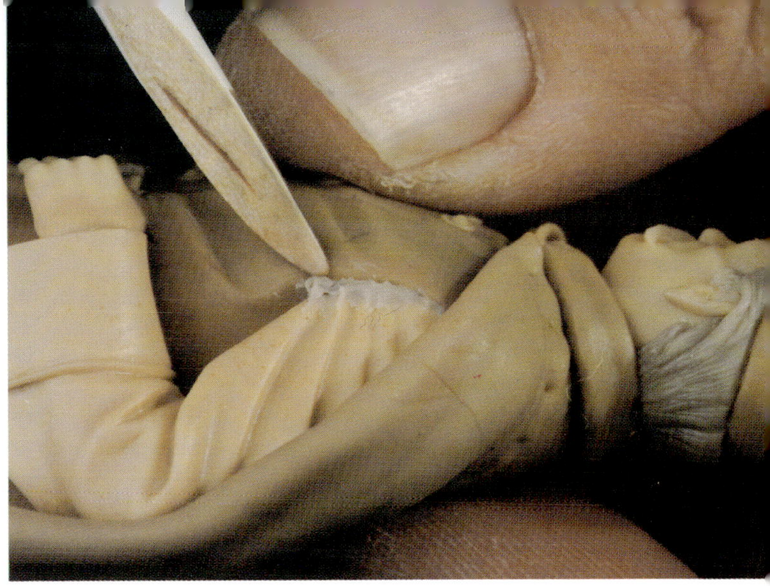

Fill the seams where the arms are attached with small rolls of putty. The gap is so large we will have to reestablish the actual clothing seam line when we are done. Contouring the putty.

Using the knife, press in the seam between the arm and the body of the coat.

*Note: Super Glue can be weakened by the heat of the oven. We have only glued pieces in place which would also be covered with and reinforced by putty. That is why the legs have yet to be attached.

The new details in place.

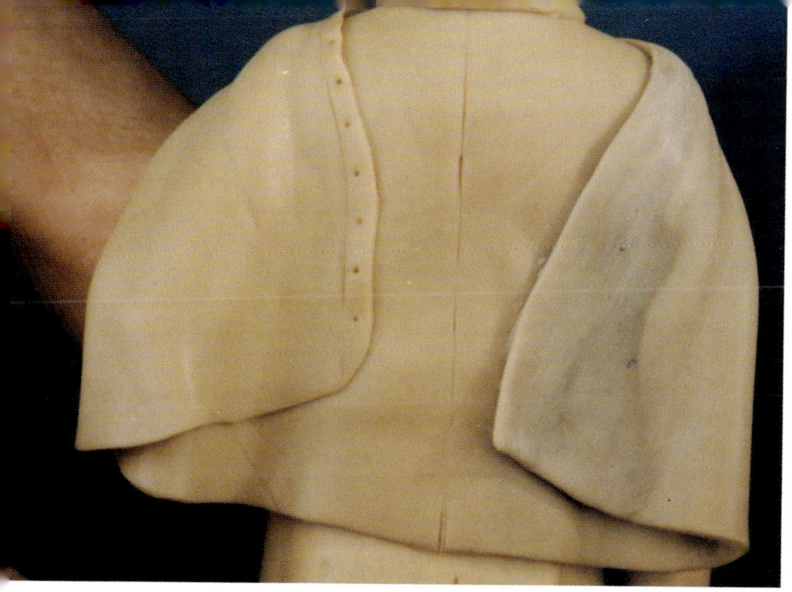

After studying the figure, I decided that the turned back portions of the cape were too flat looking. So I decided to build them up with more putty. In this photo, the right side has been fixed. We will work with the left side.

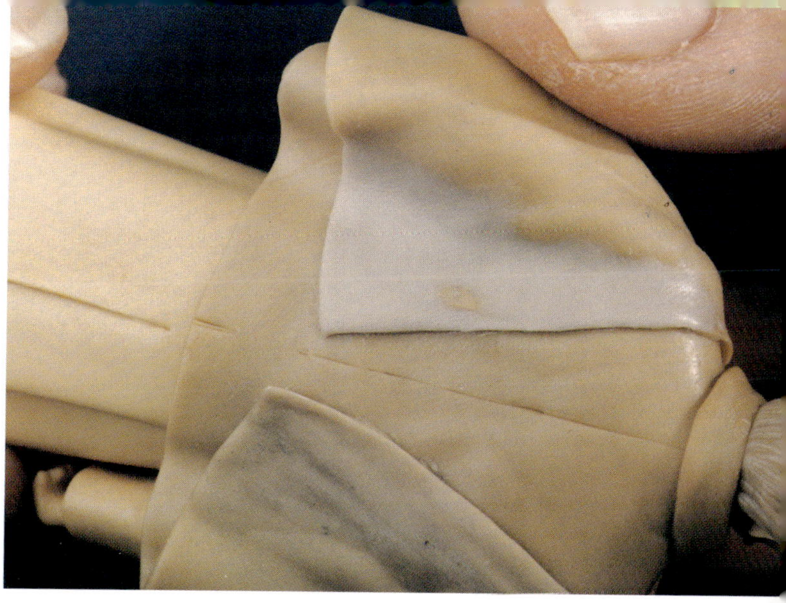

Cut away the excess with your X-acto knife.

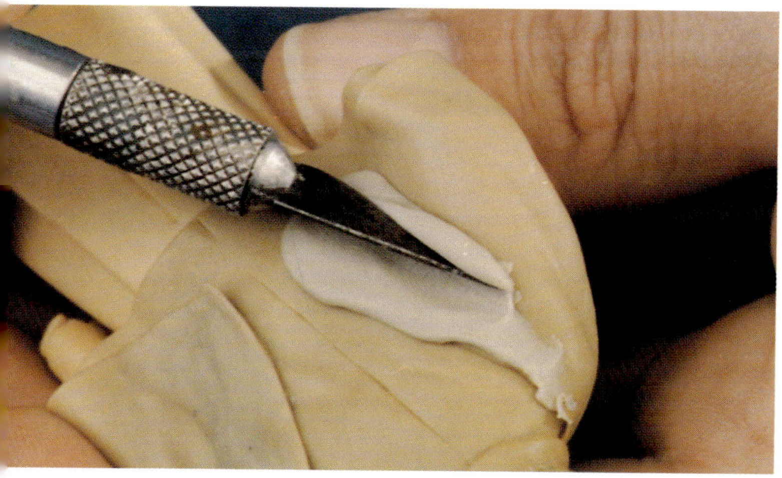

Lay in the putty and trim away the excess.

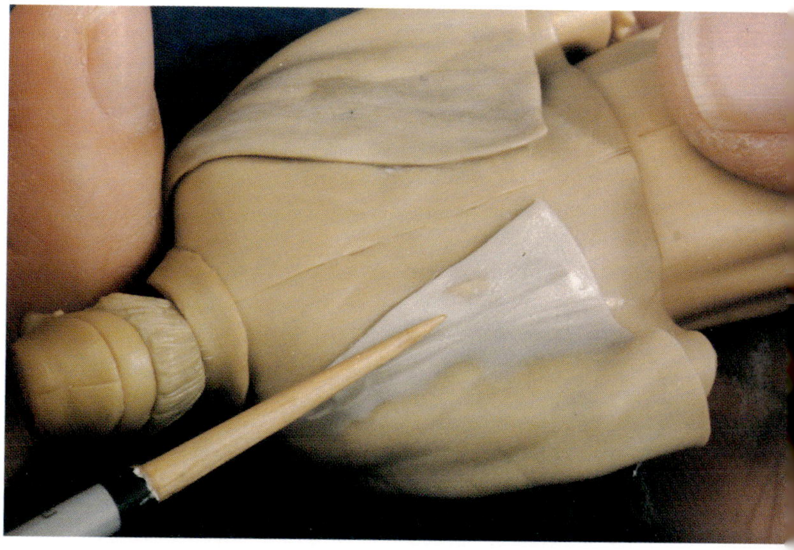

Putting in the wrinkles. Smooth them out with a brush.

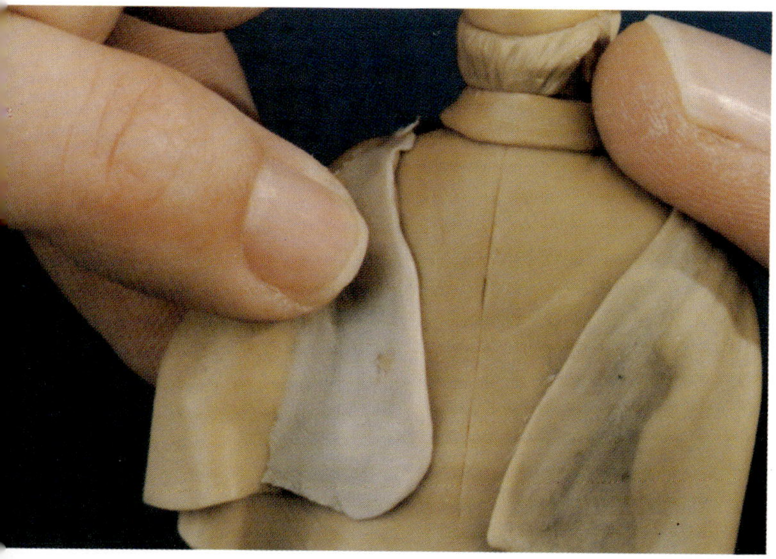

Smooth the new putty into the existing cape. Get it as smooth as possible. Once it has dried you can further smooth the putty by sanding or scraping.

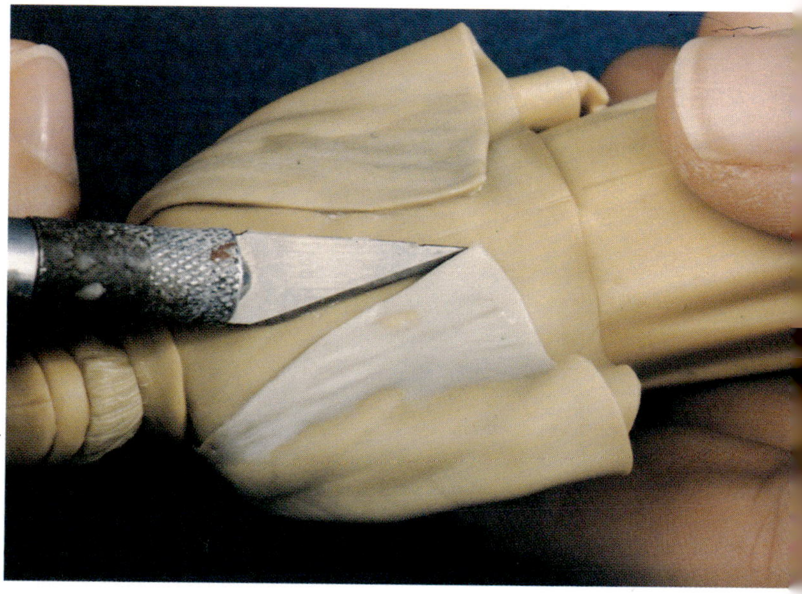

Raise the corner of the cape to show dimension. Use a gentle lifting motion. Straighten up the edge again with a moistened brush.

Add button holes.

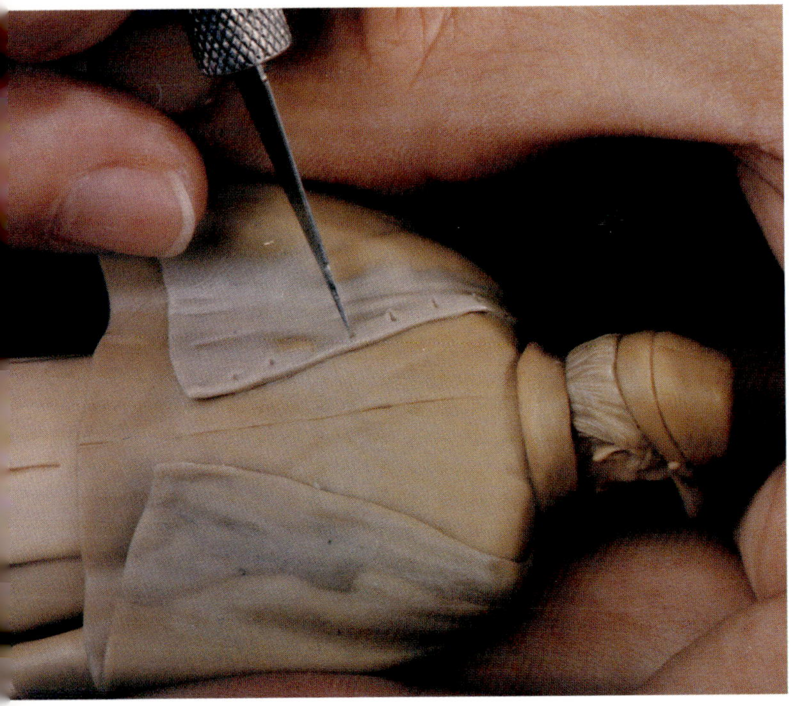

Creating the actual button holes.

Put in the hint of a seam beside the button holes. Both sides finished and ready for the oven.

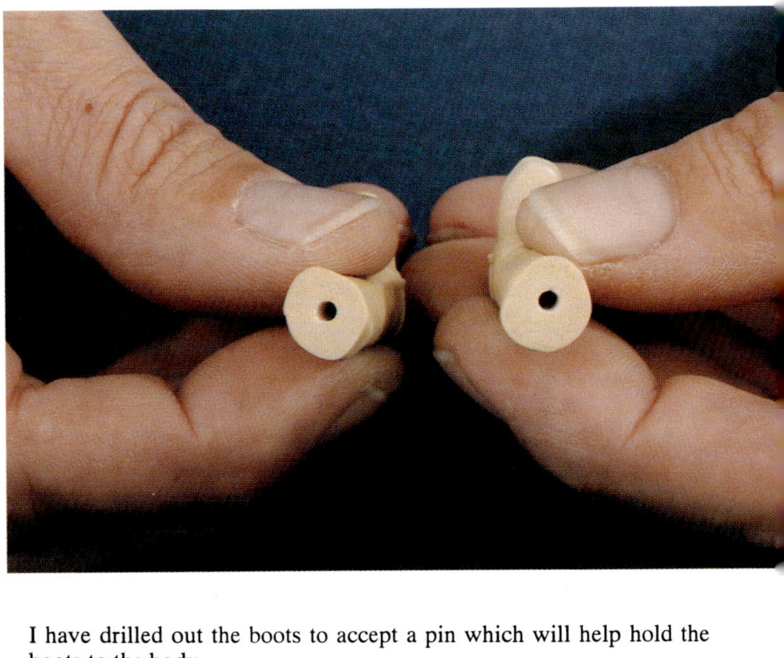

I have drilled out the boots to accept a pin which will help hold the boots to the body.

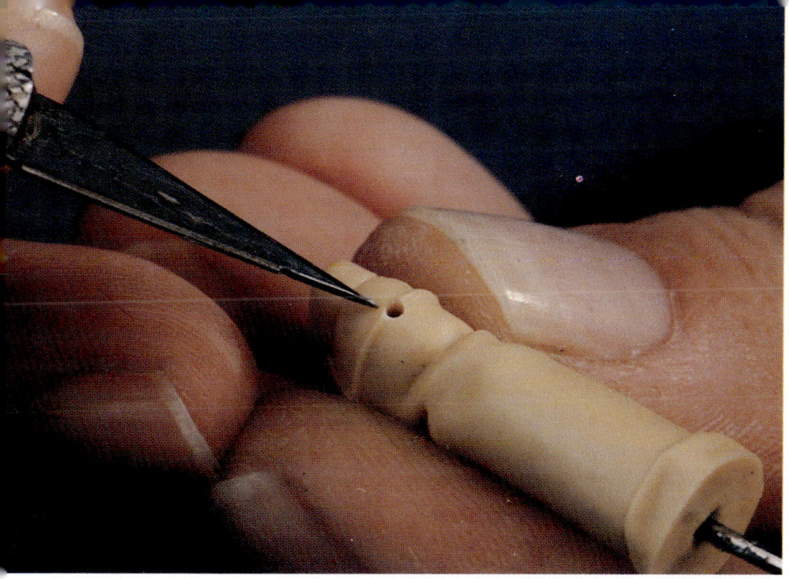

Insert a rod smaller than the hole into each boot. The extra space allows for an adequate amount of Super Glue to secure the rods. Drill out the back of the boot to accept the spur rowel as well.

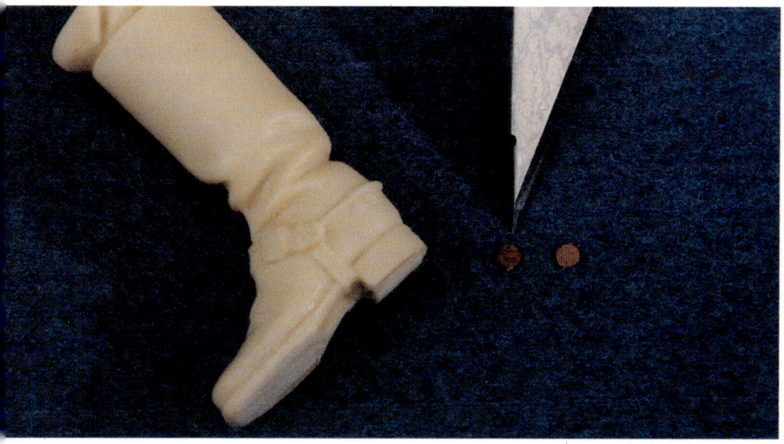

To make the spurs, first I cut two small circles from thin copper sheet metal.

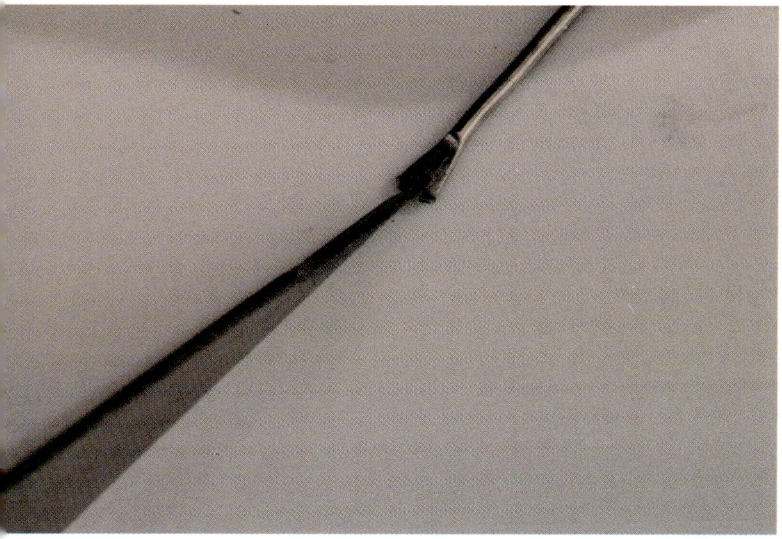

Take thin wire solder, flatten the solder tip with the back of the X-acto knife. With a very sharp blade, slice through the middle of the flattened solder tip.

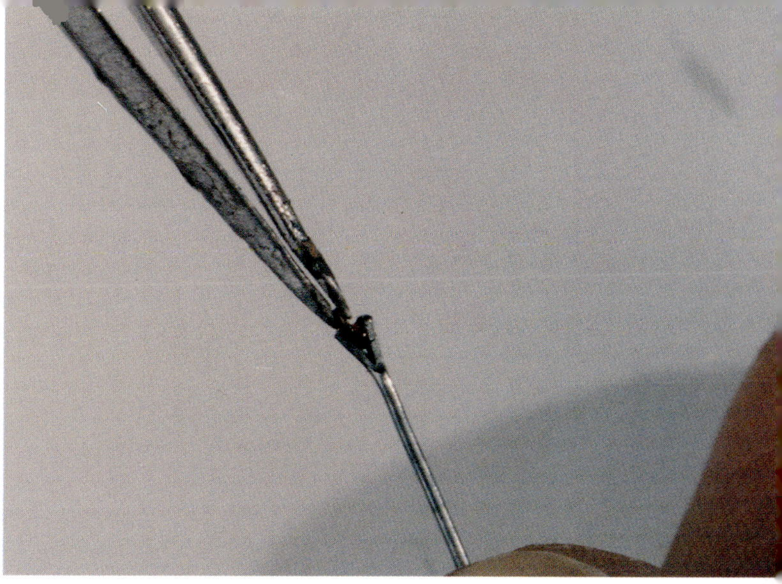

Take a small copper disk and glue it into the slit in the solder. Apply glue to the solder slit first. Insert the copper disks into the slits.

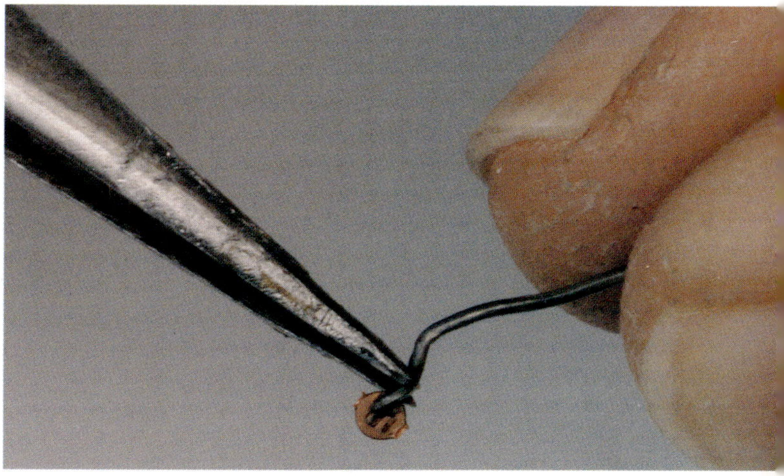

Put in the bends in the spurs so they will angle upward.

The completed spurs.

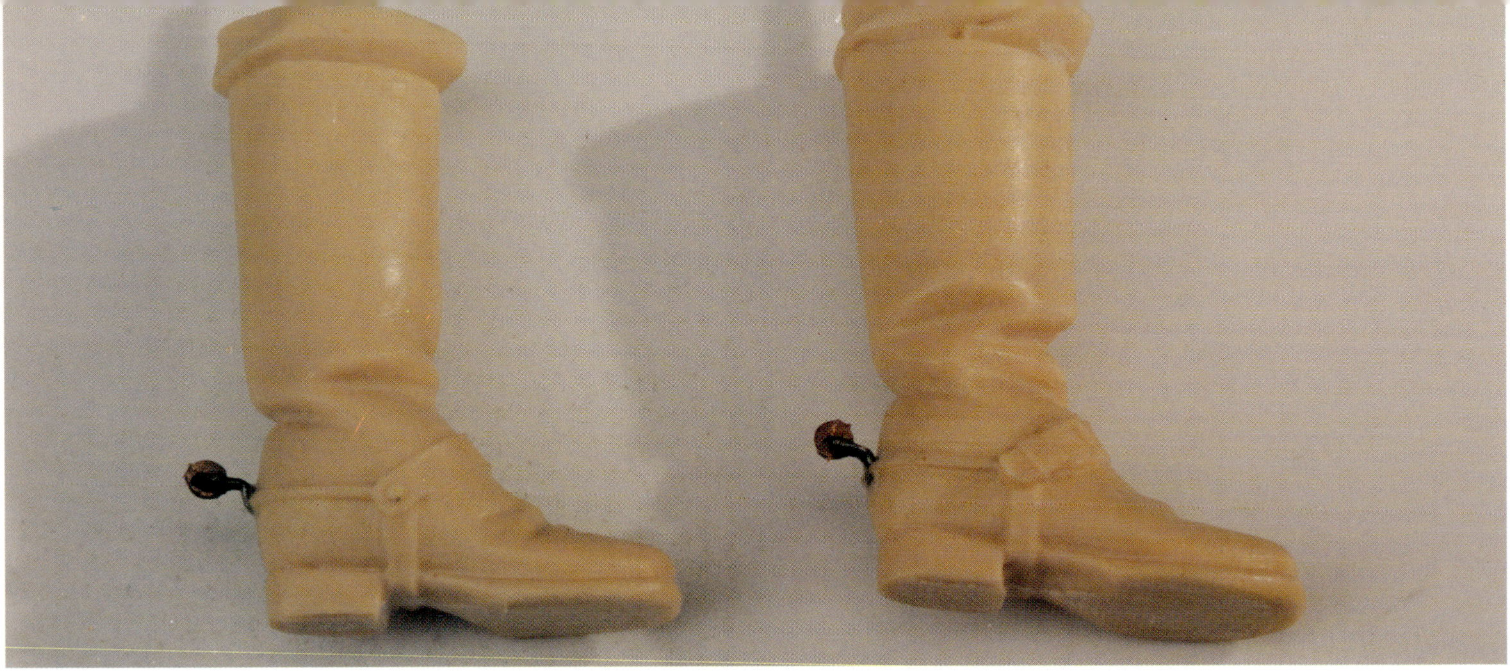

Insert the spurs into the boots, curving upward.

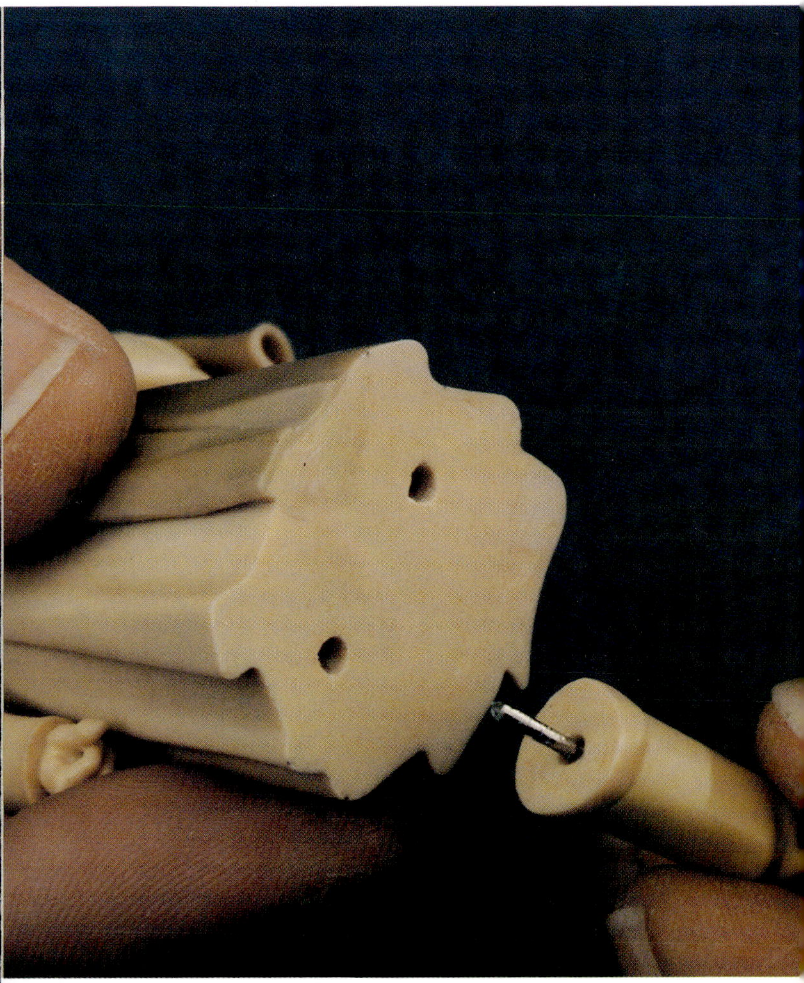

We have drilled holes into the figure to accept the pins in the legs as well. To determine where to drill the holes, take each boot one at a time, hold it up to the figure looking at it from as many angles as possible and determine the proper position. Mark around the leg on the figure with pencil or scriber. Drill the hole approximately in the center of that area. The fact that we use a pin that is smaller than the corresponding hole allows you to make minor adjustments when gluing.

The legs are in place. Be careful not to damage the spurs when putting the legs on.

Tips & Techniques

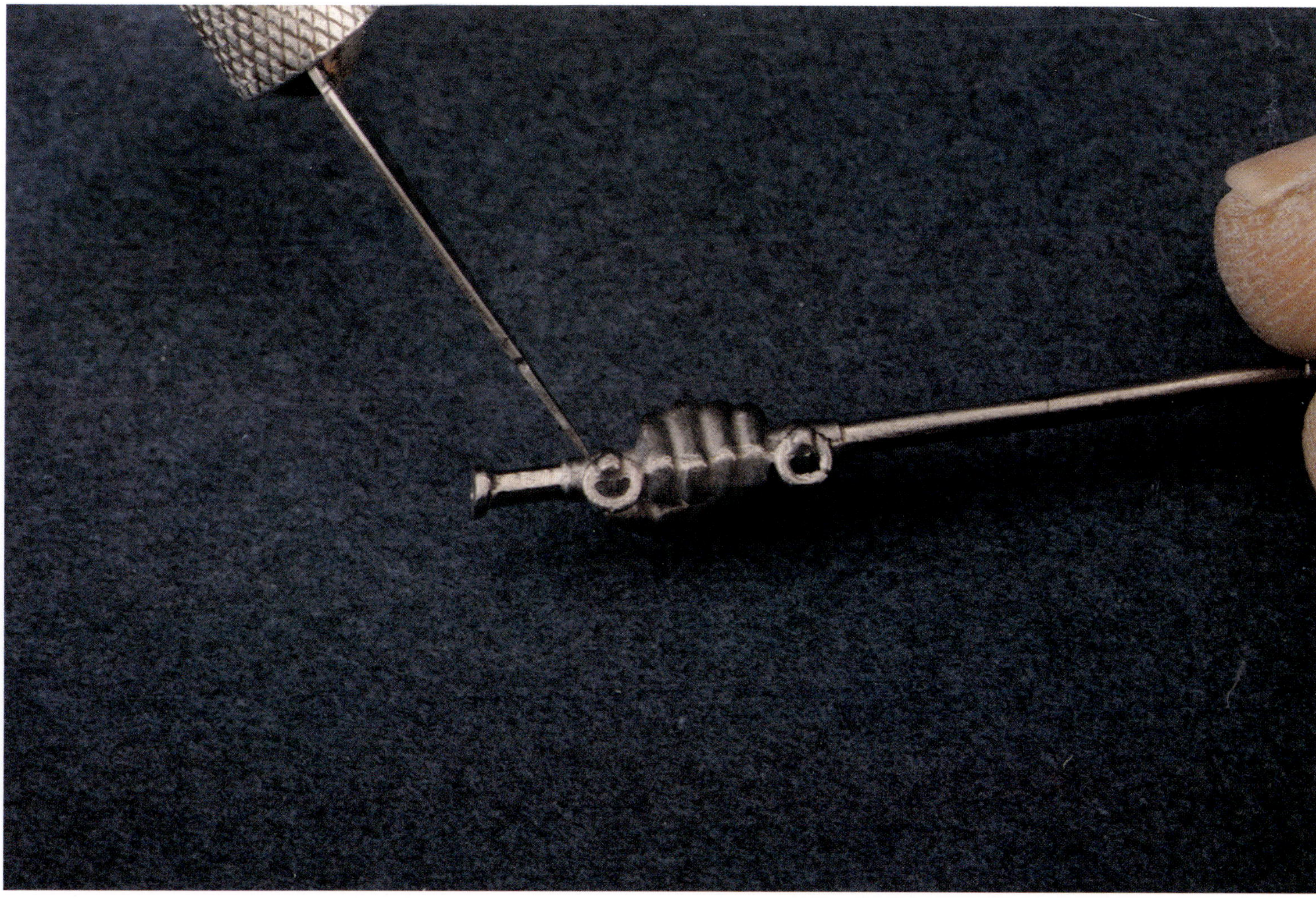

When sculpting military miniatures there are occasions when you need various sized rings such as those found on this scabbard. To make these rings you need a round object. Brass tubing of the appropriate circumference works well. You also need either fine wire or wire solder.

Opposite page photos:

Glue the holster in place and you have the finished figure. When you can't always find the figure that you would like, keep in mind that you can find one close and convert it into exactly what you want.

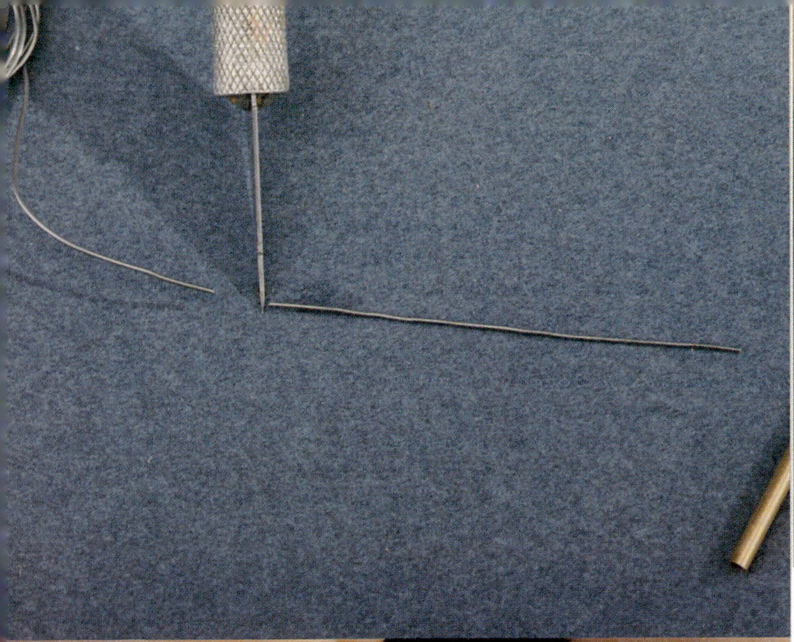

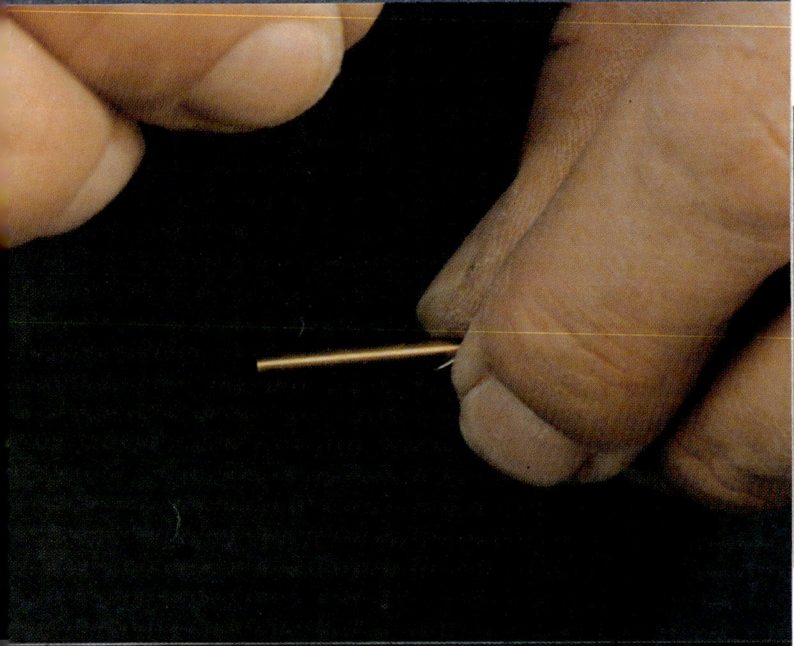

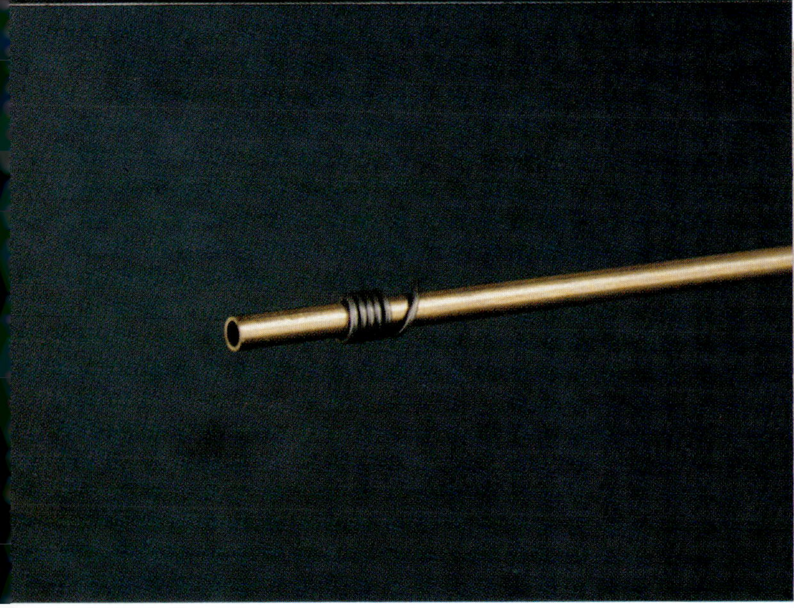

Cut off a length of wire or solder and wrap it tightly around the rod, keeping each turn as close to the last as possible.

Slide the wire or solder off of the rod and slip the tip of a sharp X-acto knife into the wire or solder coil. Cut through the coil, cutting down against a solid surface.

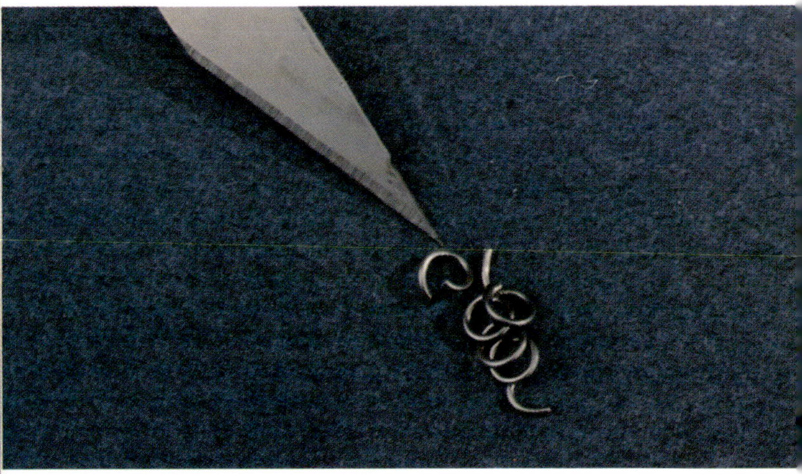

Now you have a pile of rings.

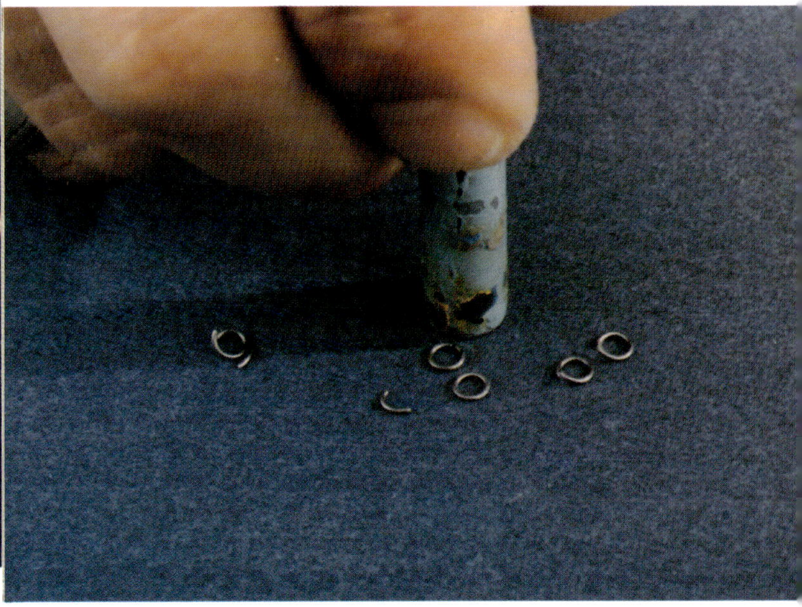

Flatten the rings with the base of the X-acto knife.

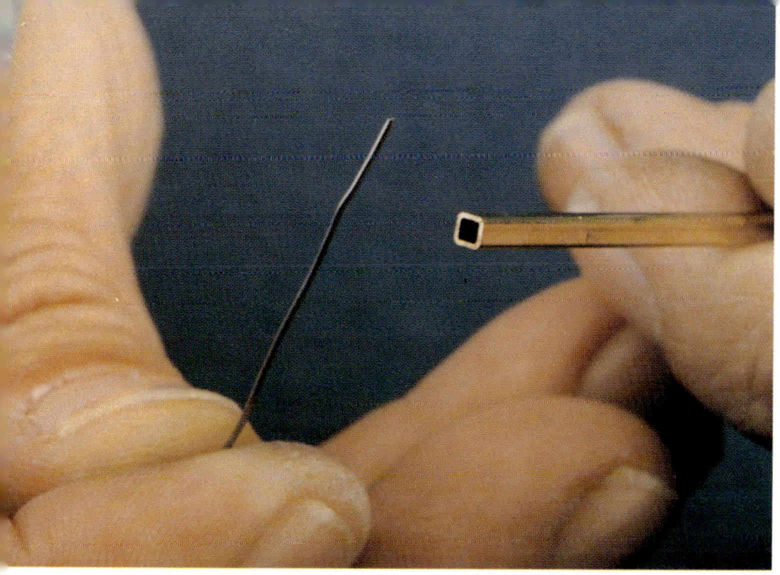

You can make buckles using the same technique with square brass tubing and solder.

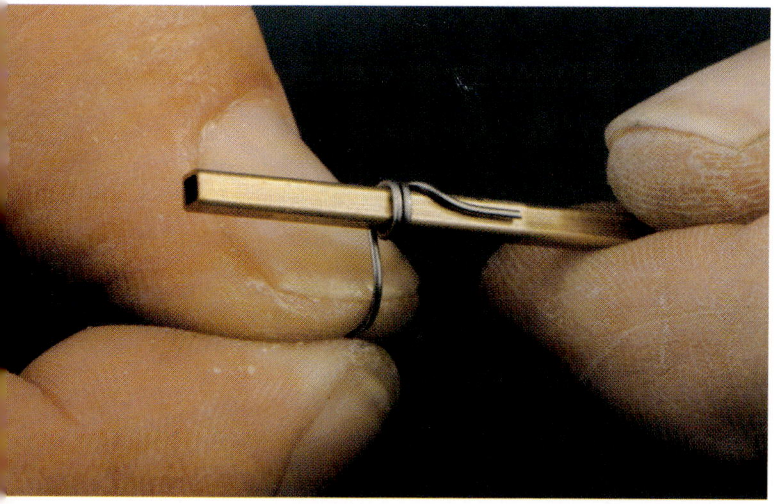

Wrap the solder (or wire) around the square tubing as tightly as possible, keeping each successive wrap as close to the previous ones as you can.

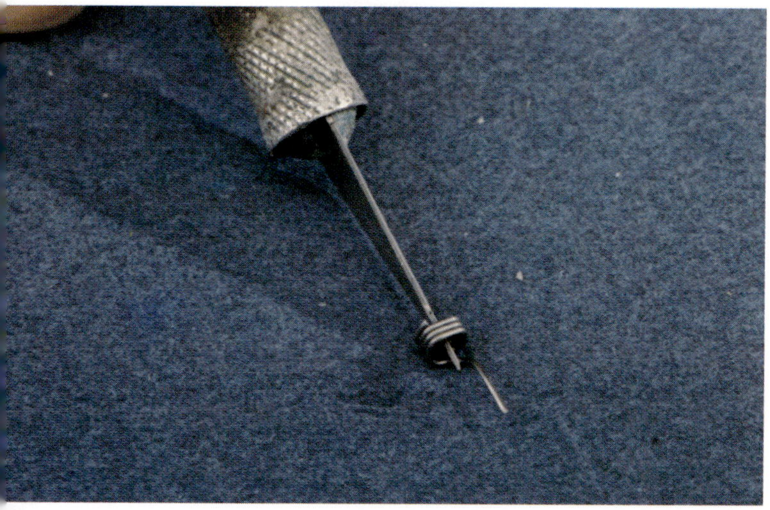

Remove the wrapped solder, insert the X-acto knife tip again and cut against a hard surface.

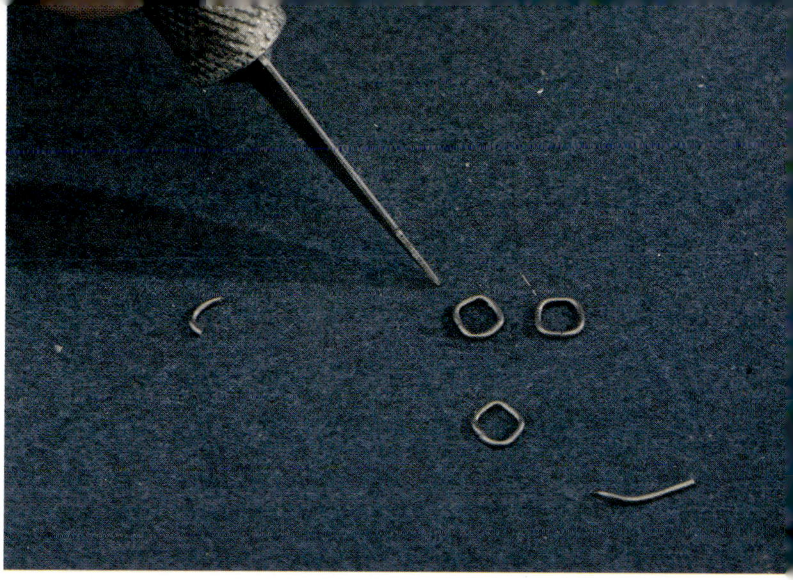

Now you have buckles. Flatten them with the base of your X-acto knife as well and they are ready.

You can also make a tool for sculpting buckles by using two consecutive sizes of square brass tubing in the appropriate scale.

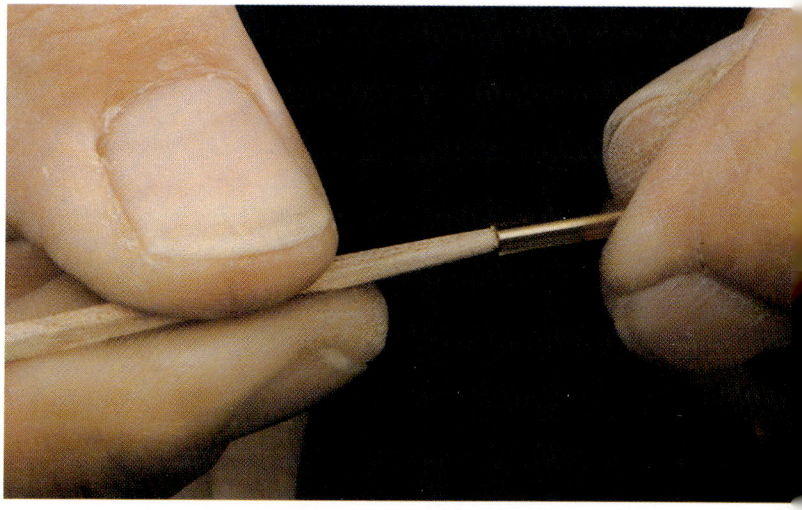

The first step is to fill the void in the smaller of the two pieces of square brass tubing with anything that will fit ... from plastic, to wood, to hardened epoxy putty.

Using a small round needle file, file in one direction on the end of the plugged tube until it is somewhat concave.

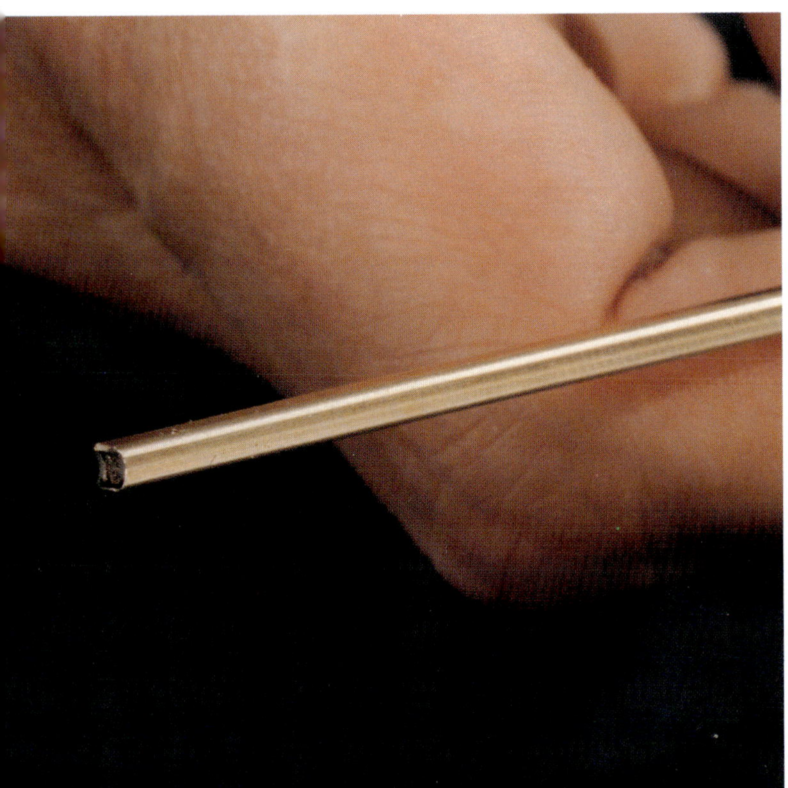

Like so.

Mark the smaller tube to an exact measurement for cutting, whate you want that length to be. Keep in mind that this will be the lengt the tool, so make it comfortable for yourself. Cut the tube off at line.

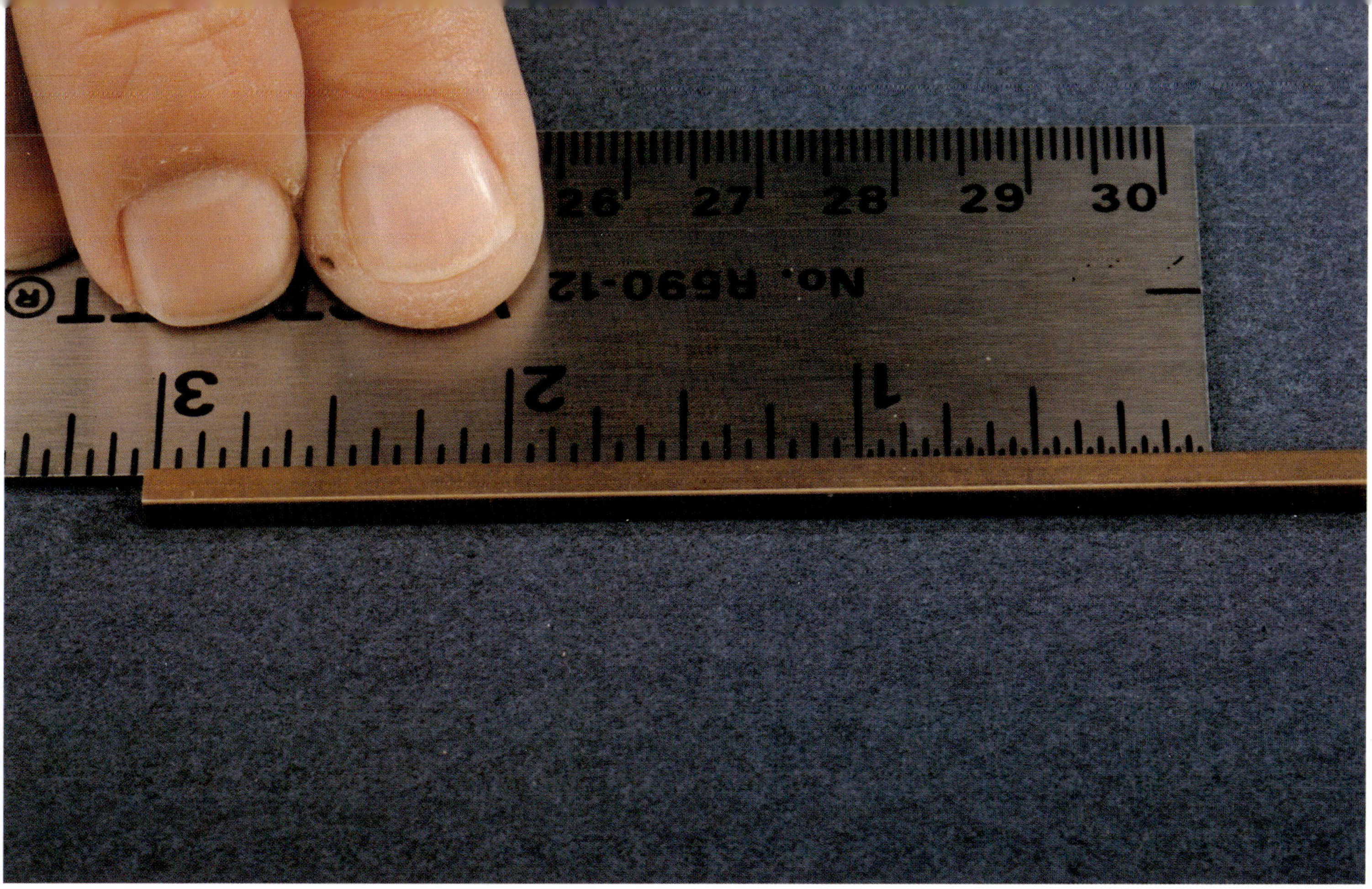

Measure the larger tube, making it 1/32 of an inch longer than the smaller tube. Mark and cut it as well.

Using a piece of emory cloth, remove the rough edges from the two tubes.

Sliding the smaller tube inside of the larger tube, add a touch of Super Glue at the end opposite to the concave end and slide the smaller tube in until it is flush with the end of the larger tube.

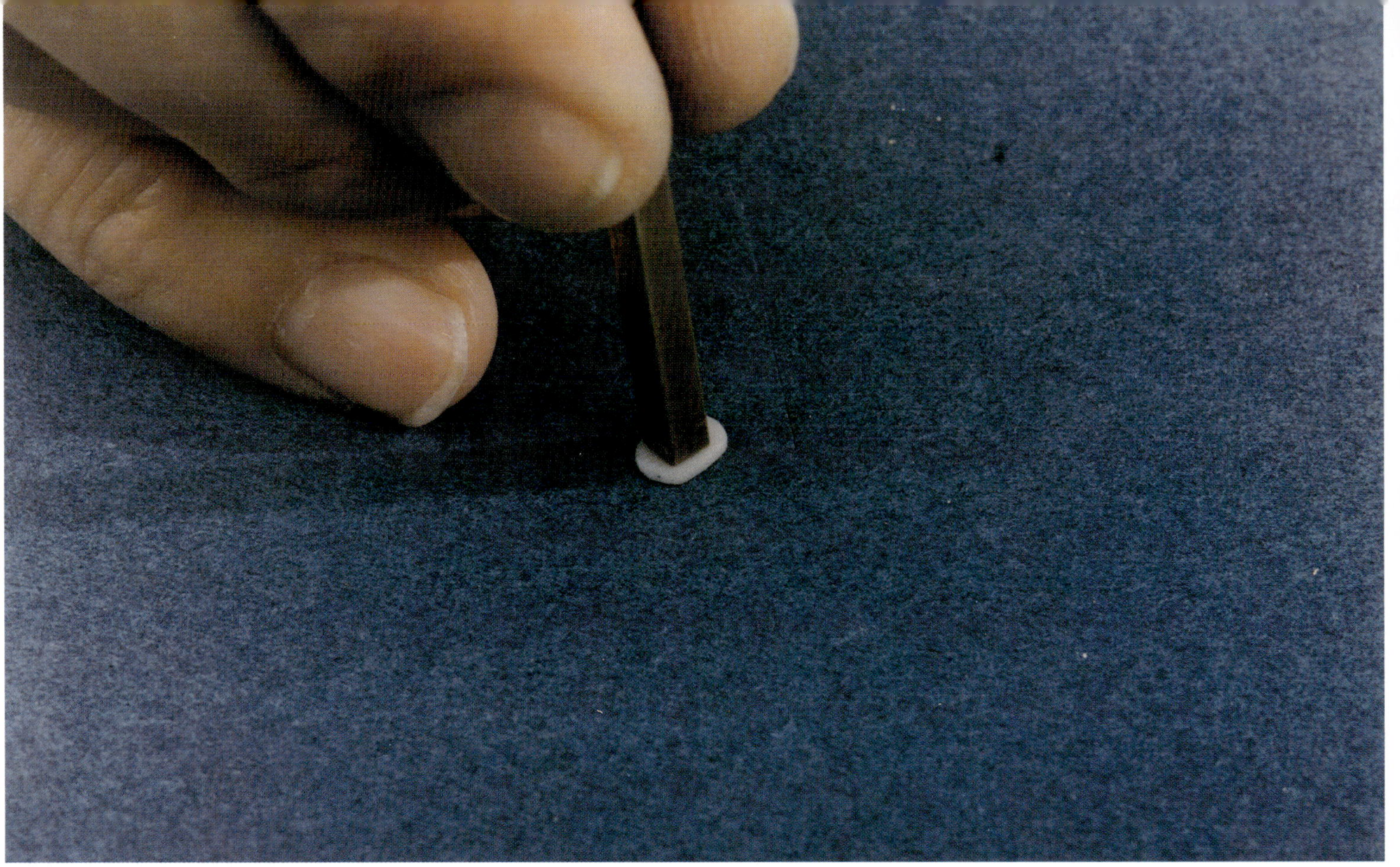

Flatten out a ball of epoxy putty on your work surface. Press the business end (the concave end) of the tool into the putty until it cuts the outside edge, almost like a cookie cutter.

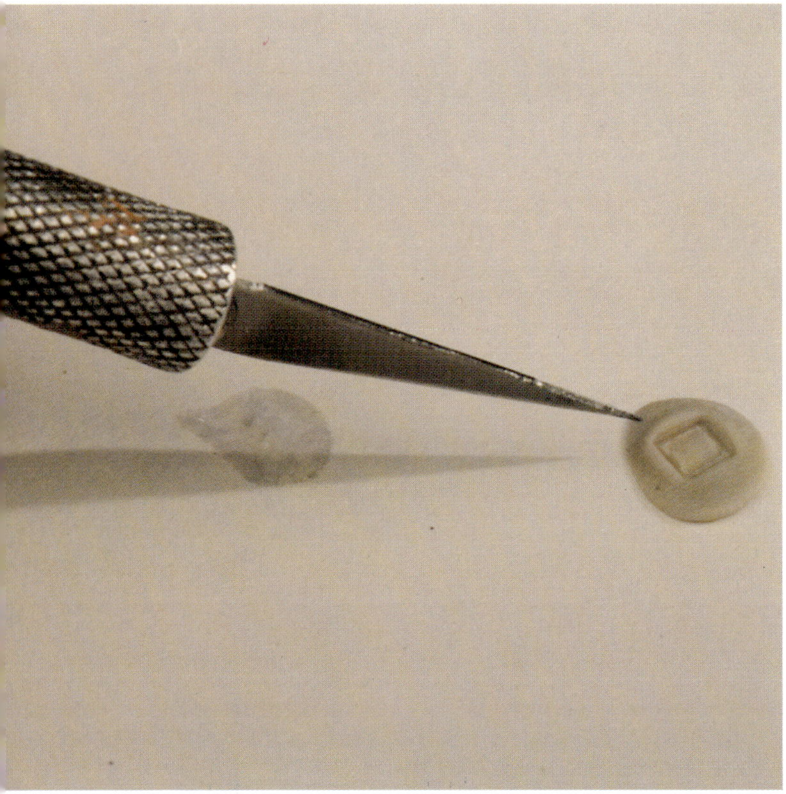

After pushing the tool into the epoxy putty trim off the excess with an X-acto knife.

The finished buckle after trimming. By varying the sizes or shapes of the tubing, you can create nearly every buckle size that you may need.

After you have completed the conversion of your figure, you will want to give some thought to how it should be displayed and what sort of terrain will surround it. It would be inappropriate to take a figure of a 19th century cavalryman and put him in a tropical forest. Therefore, some thought and planning must go into the final display base. The best place for reference material (if you don't have first hand knowledge of the terrain in which your figure fought) are photographs, illustrations, and even the texts of books. These will give you some idea of the appropriate terrain. Having visited several of the Western forts, I have seen that it was not uncommon for the men to have built rock sidewalks in front of officers' quarters and enlisted mens' barracks so I have chosen to display my trooper at one of these Western posts standing on such a rock sidewalk, perhaps contemplating the day to come. I have also seen in use at these Western forts, concrete posts with iron rings on the front to which the men would tie their horses so I have decided to model just such a scene. Here is the scene prior to painting. The figure has yet to be glued in place.

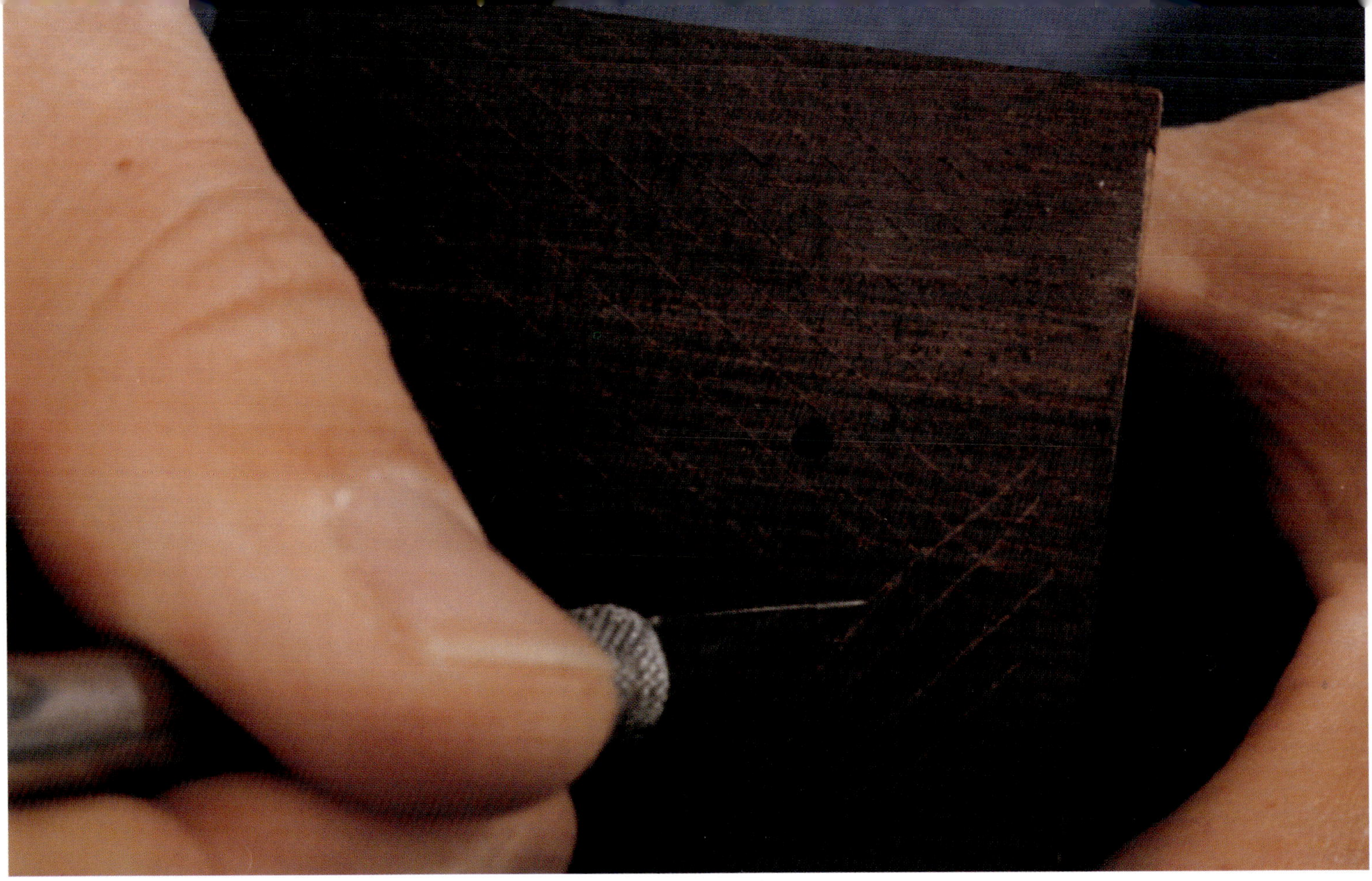

I'll begin the display base by cross-hatching the surface to help my groundwork material to adhere to it.

For larger projects that require extensive terrain I use Cell-U-Clay, a paper-mache product. It requires an armature to build up higher areas and it has a long drying time. For this project I will use epoxy putty because it is a small and relatively flat area. First insert a brass rod or toothpick into the mounting hole so that the epoxy putty will not fill it.

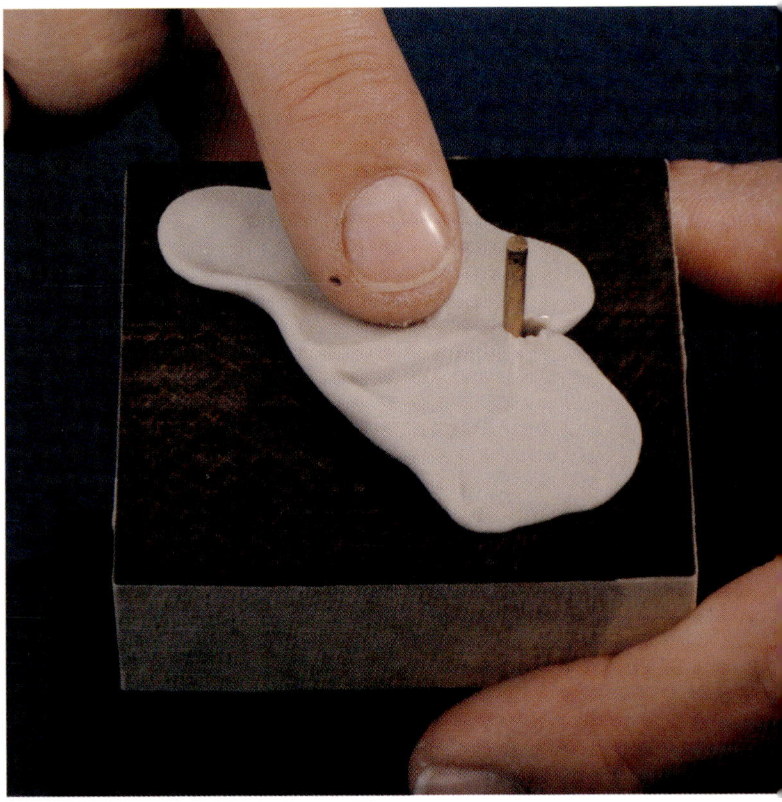

Apply masking tape to the top edge of the base to keep the putty from marring the surface of your base. Push out the epoxy putty on the base with a moistened finger.

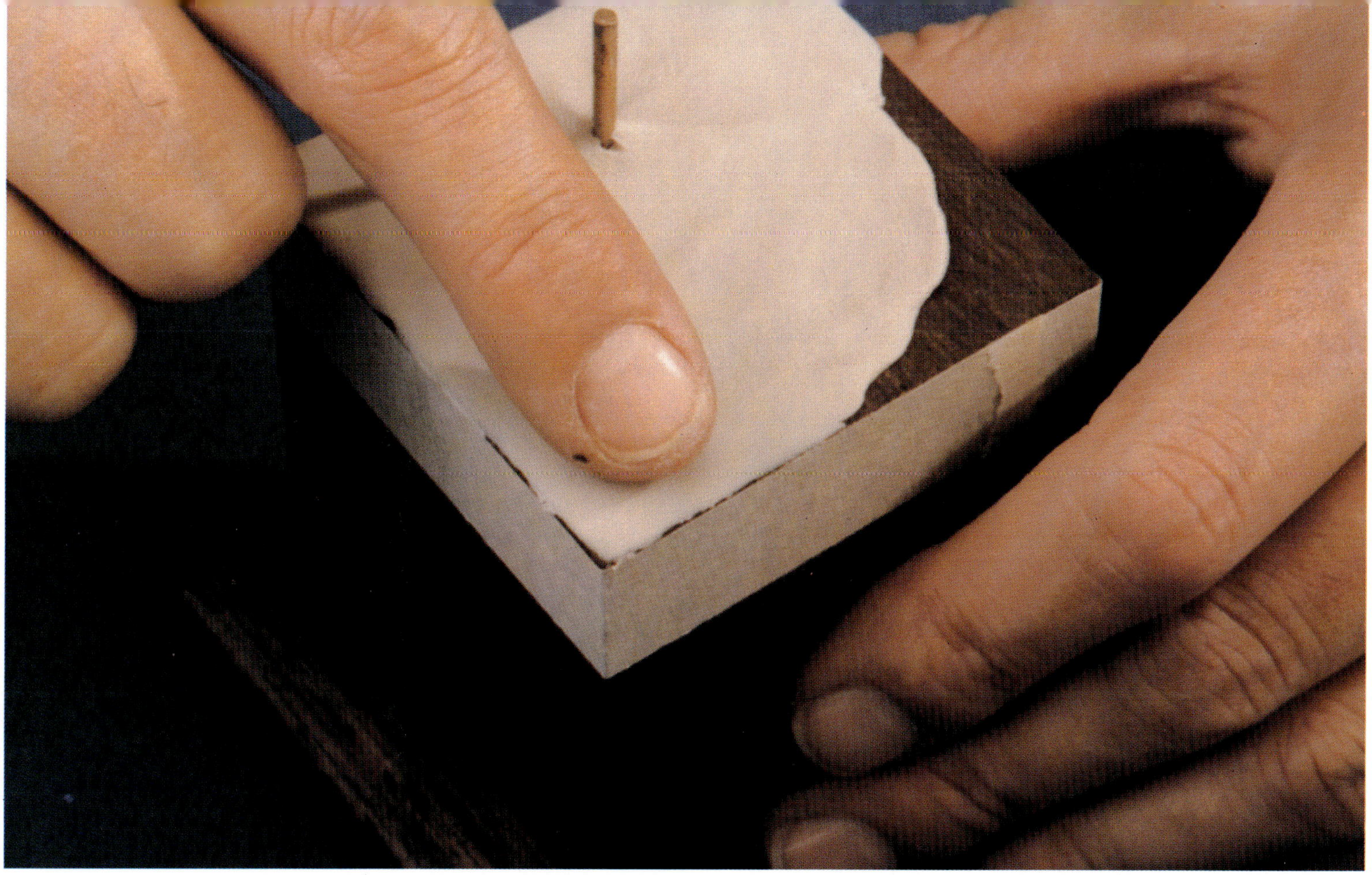

While spreading the epoxy putty, be sure that when you approach the edges of the base that the putty blends in at the same level as the top of the base. Otherwise the ground work will look stilted, as if it were not actually part of the base.

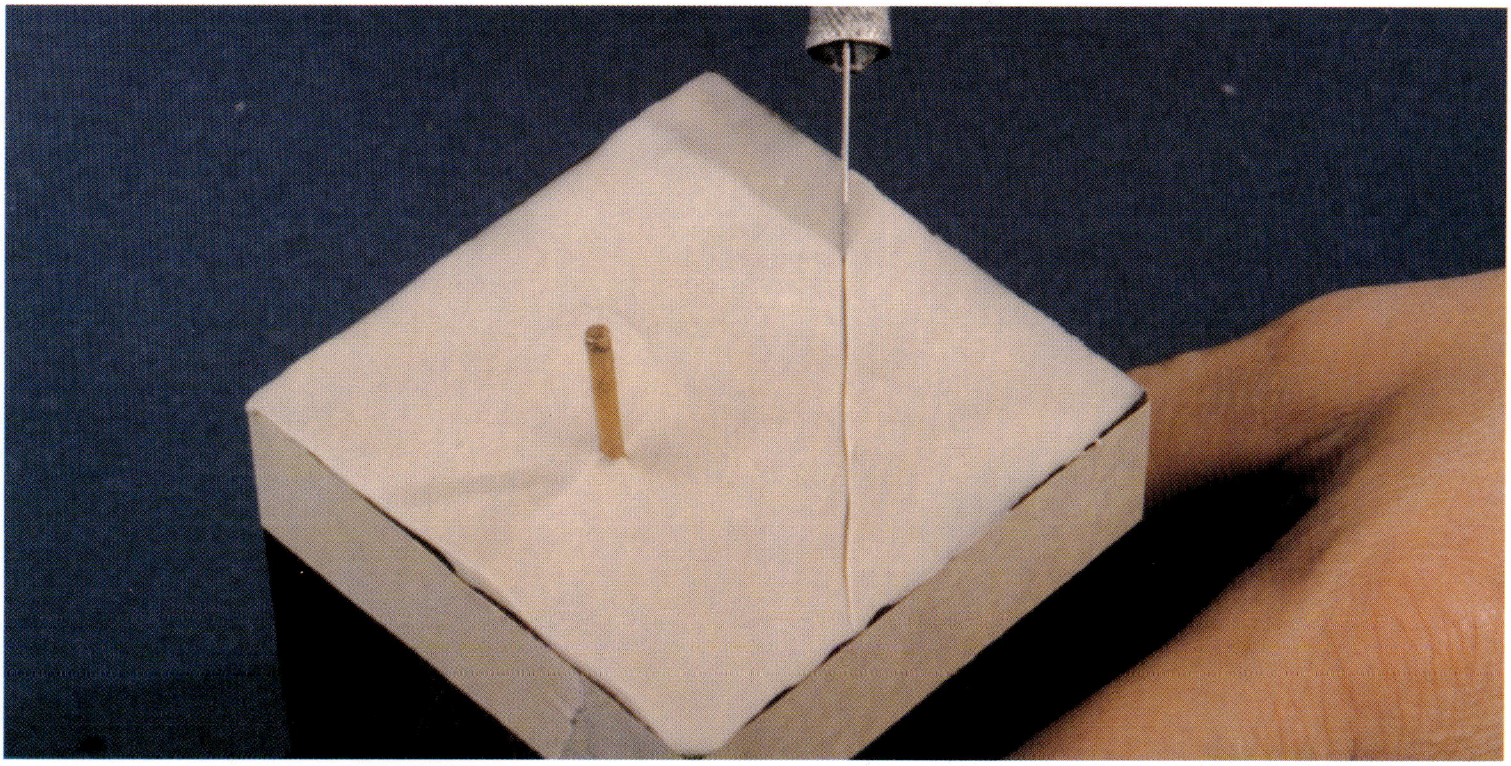

This line will be the demarcation line between the sidewalk and the edge of the parade ground. Since we want the sidewalk to have a little bit of a higher level, we'll work away the "dirt" from it somewhat. The smallest quarter area is for the parade ground grass and the hitching post.

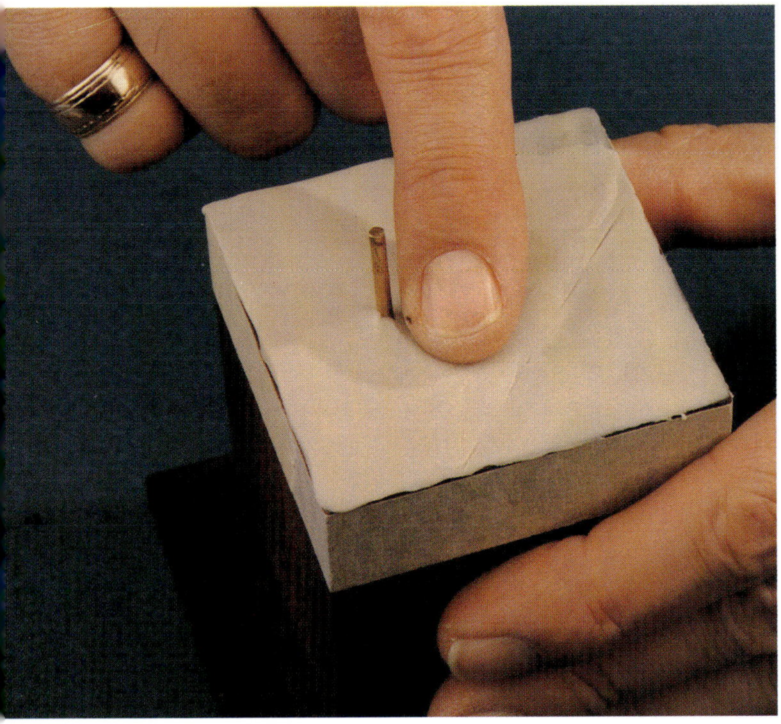

Push the bulk of the sidewalk putty toward the demarcation line between the sidewalk and the parade grounds to create the effect of a higher elevation.

Using the stylus tool, create flagstones using a random pattern. Be aware that each stone was individually placed and that they don't necessarily have to fit neatly together.

Press gently into the surface of the flagstones with a real rock to add texture. Turn the rock constantly to avoid repeating a particular pattern. Don't make the flagstones too rough because in reality they would have been selected to be used as flagstones for their flatness.

Press the rock into the groundwork as well to create texture.

The impressed surface.

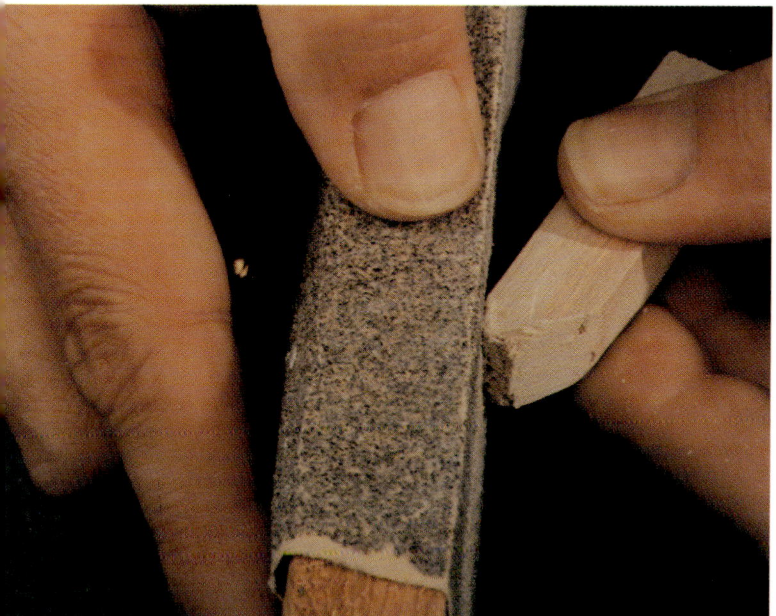

Using balsawood, I next begin work on the hitching post. I want it to be an obilisk shape so I begin by sanding a slant on two sides of the top.

Constantly check the post while sanding to be sure that the angles are the same.

Sand the other two sides as well.

Since we don't want dirt to be embedded in our flagstones, I've used an index card to cover that area.

Press the hitching post into the ground work for location. Leave it there until we add some dirt to the parade ground.

Gently sprinkle actual dirt (that has been dried and roughly ground) over the surface of the parade ground.

Remove the hitching post. Gently press down the dirt into the parade ground while avoiding the area of the hitching post.

I have divided a line of putty into four equal parts and will begin to cover the hitching post. I've found, when covering wood of any type with epoxy putty, that the putty will stick better if the wood is moistened with water or lacquer thinner.

Remove the index card and put the base in the oven to bake.

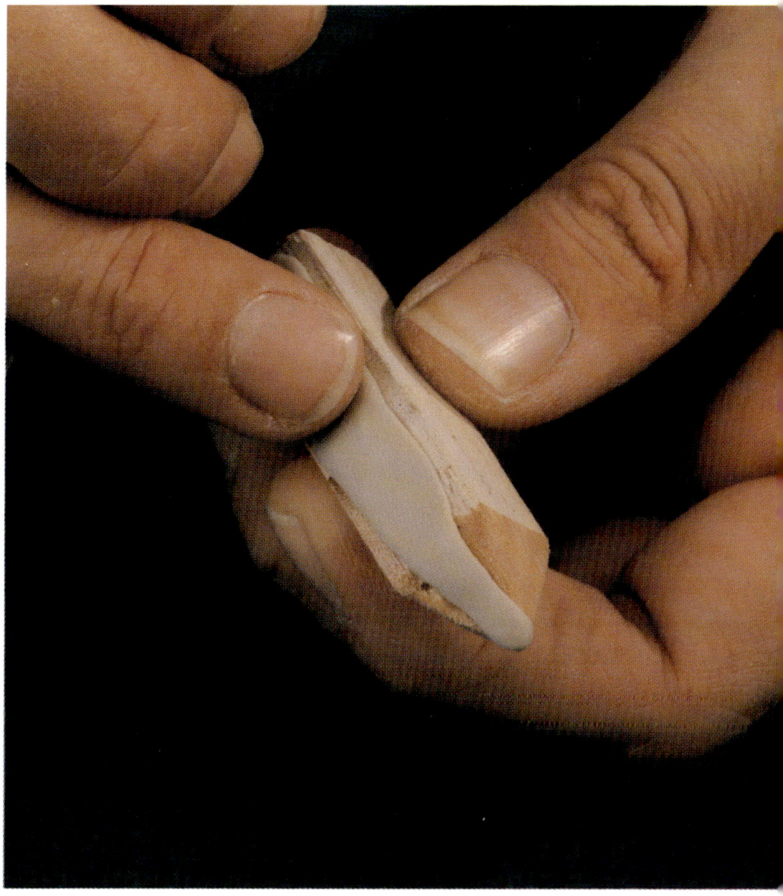

Applying the putty.

Using the tip of an X-acto knife, I'll work Super Glue into the cracks between the rocks, a few cracks at a time.

Sprinkle dirt into the cracks in the flagstones to adhere to the wet Super Glue.

After the hitching post has dried, sand the four sides and the top until smooth. If pits and cracks begin to form while sanding, don't worry because we will use them to our advantage as signs of an aging, weathered concrete post.

Drill holes in three sides of the post to attach bridle rings.

Using ring pliers, I made three U shaped pieces on which to hang the bridle rings. Make three rings using the techniques previously described.

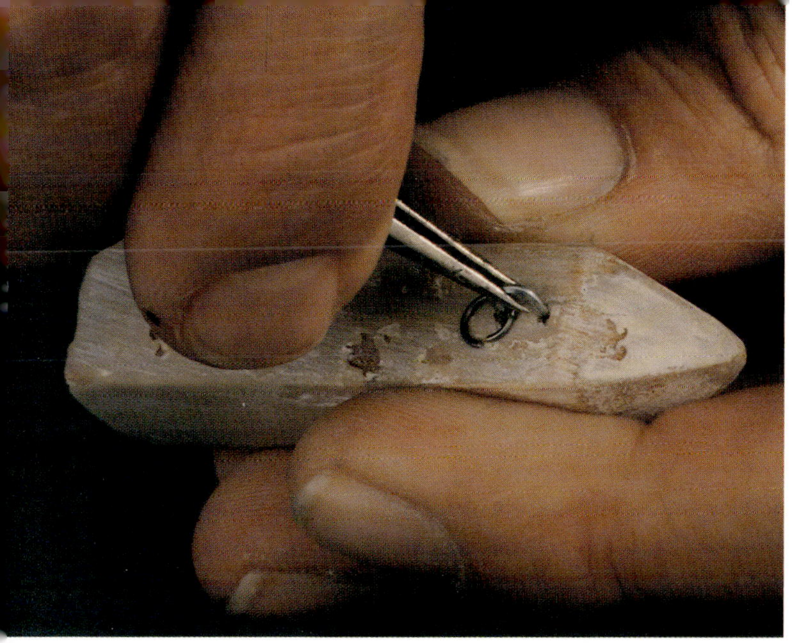

Slip the U shaped pieces through the rings and push them into the holes in the hitching post.

Once the hitching rings are set, glue the hitching post in place.

Next I'll add some grass using a piece of unraveled hemp rope.

I want the grass to be short in appearance. Cut the smallest clumps possible and apply using Super Glue. The longest grass would naturally be around the hitching post. Shorter grass would be found away from the post where foot traffic would wear it down.

The grass before trimming.

The trimmed grass.

While I have not glued the figure to the base yet, as I need to paint it first, here is the converted figure and its base.

More photos of the converted figure and its base.

The Gallery

"First Sgt. Mexican Punitive Expedition, 1916."

"Bugler, 1st Rgt. U.S. Dragoons, 1854."

"GI Jenny. The Pride of the 5th."

"The Avenging Angel."

"Joe D. Maguire." *From the Collection of Jon Maguire.*

The completed U.S. cavalryman. *Painted by Mike Davidson.*